The Psychoanalyst in Psychiatry

The Psychoanalyst in Psychiatry

Thomas Freeman

Yale University Press
New Haven

616.89
F 855 p

First published in Great Britain 1988 by H. Karnac (Books) Ltd.
Published in the United States 1988 by Yale University Press.

Printed in Great Britain.
Produced by Free Association Books, London.

Library of Congress Cataloging-in-Publication Data

Freeman, Thomas.
  The psychoanalyst in psychiatry.

  Includes bibliographies and index.
  1. Psychoanalysis. I. Title. [DNLM: 1. Mental
Disorders. 2. Psychoanalytic Theory. WM 460 F8552p]
RC504.F66 1988   616.89'17   87-10684
ISBN 0-300-04071-7

10   9   8   7   6   5   4   3   2   1

CONTENTS

	Acknowledgements	vi
	Foreword	viii
	Introduction	1
1.	On Transitivism and Appersonation	7
2.	Nosographic Aspects of Schizophrenic and Paranoid Psychoses	14
3.	Nosography and the Course of Schizophrenic and Paranoid Psychoses	35
4.	Pre-psychotic Identifications and their Vicissitudes in the Schizophrenias	49
5.	The Contents of Delusions and Hysterical Phantasies	59
6.	The Delusion of Persecution by a Known Person of the Opposite Sex	79
7	Psychoanalytic Aspects of Organic Mental States	87
8.	Notes on Neurotic Symptoms	107
9.	A Childhood Orientation in Adult Psychiatry	115
10.	A Developmental Theory of Psychoses	126
11.	The Psychoanalytic Treatment of a Borderline State	136
12.	Treatment of the Psychoses	144
	Appendix: The Psychoanalytic Examination of a Psychotic State	166
	References	184
	Index	194

ACKNOWLEDGEMENTS

I WISH to thank my wife for the idea of writing this book and for typing the manuscript. I also thank Dr John Gottlieb MD of Chicago for the work he did with the patient (Wilson) whose case is described in Chapter 3 and in the Appendix. I am also indebted to Ann Scott of Free Association Books for her helpful suggestions and for the interest she has taken in the book. Acknowledgement is made to the editor of the *International Review of Psycho-Analysis* for permission to reprint the paper 'The Psychoanalytic Examination of a Psychotic State' in the Appendix.

'. . . it remains true that in scientific matters it is always experience, and never authority without experience, that gives the final verdict, whether in favour or against.'

Freud (1888), Preface to the Translation of Bernheim's *Suggestion*

FOREWORD

PSYCHOANALYSTS have played a prominent role in adult and child psychiatry since Sigmund Freud's discoveries, starting in the late nineteenth century, revolutionized our understanding and expectations about human development and behaviour. In recent years, there has been a shrill insistence that substantial advances of psychopharmacology and biological psychiatry have eclipsed the illuminations of psychoanalysis with regard to psychiatric patients. In this shrillness there is an unrealistic effort to polarize our theory and methods of diagnosis and treatment, an all-too-familiar human wish to simplify multi-determined phenomena into an either/or explanation of the characteristics, development and treatment of patients who are mentally ill.

This preference for either a biological or a psychodynamic approach not only moves away from the real complexity of neuroses and psychoses, it also tends to hide or obscure the way in which complementary explanations and treatments of these conditions can be mutually illuminating and helpful. When such multiple determinants as those involved in the genesis and manifestations of psychiatric illness are overlooked or are replaced by an insistence on an either/or approach to the study and treatment of such patients, a balanced understanding will not be achieved; and the secondary distorting effects of how patients are evaluated and treated will be overlooked and not taken into account.

In this splendid book, Dr Thomas Freeman has put into an illuminating and useful synthesis his superb clinical and theoretical knowledge of the phenomenological, psychoanalytic and bio-psychopharmacological aspects of psychiatric conditions. There is an understandable emphasis on the psychotic process and on the hospitalized psychiatric patient.

Utilizing case vignettes from rich and lengthy experiences of studying and treating psychiatric patients, the author moves from the surface of the patient's behaviour to the depth of the patient's inner psychic life. There is a profound scholarly message carried by this book, one that needs to be relearned periodically. Not only do our patients have self-healing capacities, but such resources can be facilitated or impaired by the way professionals approach the diagnostic and therapeutic process. Repeatedly, the author lucidly points out how and when pharmacological agents relieve and facilitate treatment and restitution; how such agents never cure; and how often such agents, if used too much or too long can interfere with and complicate the patient's recovery. The psychoanalytic approach, when misused or abused can also complicate or impair the patient's recovery, just as it can facilitate clearing the pathway to recovery when it is well used.

As in the past, psychoanalysts have much to contribute to the care and increased understanding of patients with major psychiatric disorders. However, they seem to have retreated from leadership in the treatment of the psychoses, not only because of advances in psychopharmacological treatment but also because their interests have taken them increasingly into other applied areas such as child psychotherapy, attachment and loss experiences throughout the life cycle, forensic psychiatry and to those opportunities for collaborative research, teaching and improved preventive services that advances in ego psychology have provided.

This book is an inviting reminder that as psychoanalysts, in collaboration with biological psychiatrists, we have promising opportunities to enlarge our knowledge and to improve the care of patients with major psychiatric disorders. The scholarly clinical perspectives in this volume also constructively return us to an essential focus, that of the natural course of psychiatric disorders. How do our diagnostic and therapeutic procedures and agents influence the course of illness and recovery? What are the differences between the pathogenic and restitutive responses by patients with major psychiatric disorders? Such questions imply what this book demonstrates, that an integrative view of body/mind functioning is our best hope for understanding and effectively treating psychiatric patients.

Albert J. Solnit, MD
Sigmund Freud Professor of
Psychoanalysis at Hebrew
University of Jerusalem and
Sterling Professor of Pediatrics
and Psychiatry, Child Study
Center, Yale University

INTRODUCTION

THIS BOOK describes the psychoanalytic approach to the clinical problems encountered in psychiatric practice. This approach is not merely a matter of theoretical conceptualization or of therapeutic aspiration, but is rather in the nature of a clinical discipline which, over the years, virtually unnoticed, has widened and refined the range of clinical observation (Jung, 1907; Freud, 1911, 1915b, 1915c; Ferenczi, 1912; Nunberg, 1921; Katan, 1974, 1979); while Kety (1961) has called it a means of information retrieval. Its use is dependent on recognizing that patients do not easily reveal their innermost thoughts and feelings; and that this resistance, in the case of the psychoses, takes unpredictable and delusional forms (see Chapters 3 and 4, the cases of William and Roberta). There is little chance of overlooking this fact of resistance when there is an opportunity to engage in regular psychoanalytic work with patients suffering from symptom and character neuroses.

Other benefits are to be gained by moving from the neurotic patient to the psychotic patient and vice versa, for this concurrent work confirms the oft-reported observation that the wishes and fears of the psychotic and non-psychotic patient are basically identical. The difference in the patient's subjective experiences can be attributed to the manner in which the wishes find expression: the neurotic patient blames the analyst for a thought or affect he does not like, but this response is usually transitory; the psychotic also attributes responsibility for unwanted thoughts or intentions. Here, however, there is a belief in the analyst's malevolence, which often cannot be dissipated by interpretation or the passage of time. The ways in which the thought or wish is experienced depend on the nature of the mental organization that is extant following regression or dissolution of psychical structure. Moreover, the search for the unconscious wish which lies behind a delusional thought is often blocked by the absence of a therapeutic alliance between analyst and psychotic patient. A clue to the wish, however, sometimes presents itself during the course of the analysis of a neurotic patient. Erotomania and transference love represent this point (Freeman, 1984a), and analysis of the transference love offers a possible explanation for the emergence of the erotomania.

Over the past two or more decades descriptive studies of psychoses have suffered from the impact of chemotherapy, particularly from the long-acting medications. Chemotherapy has tended to obscure the clinical manifestations and interfere with the natural course of the illness, and it has therefore been less easy to decide whether or not the disappearance of a delusion or catatonic sign is in fact indicative of a remission of the attack. Equally, it is difficult in long-standing, chronic cases to determine whether the potential for further improvement is being hampered or assisted by the drug treatment. However, chemotherapy need not have these effects. In modest doses and in the context of an understanding relationship with psychiatrist or nurse, it is still possible, through the patients' utterances, to observe the great variation within and between types of psychosis that exists, and to follow the different courses of illnesses (see Chapters 2 and 3).

Psychoanalysts working in this field have approached the clinical phenomena in two ways. They have used them, firstly, as a foundation for theoretical constructions (see Freud, 1911; Klein, 1946); and have attempted, secondly, to order the manifestations in terms of explanatory concepts. In the former case, transitivism and appersonation (see Chapter 1) form the clinical bases of the different psychoanalytic theories of psychoses (see Freud, 1915c; Federn, 1953; Klein, 1946). The material in Chapters 2 and 3 is illustrative of the latter: here delusional contents are ordered in terms of the results of the pioneering studies of Abraham, Freud and Ferenczi. The clinical data can also be organized and classified with the aid of a psychoanalytic profile originally introduced by Anna Freud (Freud, A. et al., 1965), and modified for use with the psychoses.

A description of the schema and its use is given in the Appendix.

Chapter 5 describes the similarities which exist between the contents of hysterical phantasies and of delusions, as well as the occasion for their appearance and the psychical reactions which they evoke. However, different usages of the term phantasy (Freud, 1916; Segal, 1978) necessitate a few words of clarification. In this context the term phantasy is used to denote a complex of ideas – conscious, preconscious or unconscious – which exist independently of the constraints and requirements of reality. The content of these ideas is varied, but always of a wish-fulfilling nature (Freud, 1916); while disappointment and frustration lead to their proliferation. This is universally the case with patients suffering from hysterical neuroses (anxiety and conversion hysteria). In addition, the relationship of phantasy to consciousness depends on whether a phantasy leads to anxiety and guilt. Thus, phantasies which become conscious despite such reactions do so after their content has been transformed into a source of fear rather than pleasure.

In mental hospitals today there are no longer the large numbers of patients suffering from general paresis, epilepsy and post-encephalitic parkinsonism. Their place has been taken by cases of senile dementia, arteriosclerotic dementia and the various pre-senile dementias. Together these illnesses constitute more than 50 per cent of the mental hospital population. The psychoanalyst who chooses to participate equally with his psychiatric colleagues will inevitably find himself face to face with these organic states.

In the course of attempting to strengthen and shore up what remains to these patients of abstract thought, selective attention and short-term memory, certain phenomena are to be observed which again point to the presence of common elements in the mental life of the healthy, the neurotically afflicted, the psychotic and the brain-damaged (Freeman, 1969). Outstanding in this respect is the phenomenon of automatic (involuntary) repetition – a phenomenon also to be found in long-standing cases of schizophrenia, in epilepsy, in brain tumours and in the mentally handicapped. This automatic repetition, as will be described in Chapter 7, is operative at the most elementary and at the most advanced levels of mental organization. Its ubiquitousness points to a continuity between mental processes which, on the one hand, can barely be distinguished from somatic (neurological) processes; and the apparently autonomous cognition of the mentally healthy adult, on the other. Just as in the functional psychosis, organic mental states reveal *ad oculos* the presence of forms of mental activity which can only be inferred from the dreams of the healthy and from the free associations, phantasies and symptoms of patients suffering from neuroses.

The change in the mental hospital population has not been confined to long-stay patients. Over a period of many years there has been a gradual change in the composition of the population of admission wards. Ratcliffe (1964) reported that in Scottish mental hospitals during the years 1945–9 neurotics (excluding reactive depression), alcoholism and psychopathic personality accounted for 5% of admissions only. In the years 1955–9 these accounted for 20% of admissions. An investigation carried out by the author with two colleagues into the characteristics of female patients admitted to mental hospital on account of depressive symptoms (Freeman *et al.*, 1970) showed that 82% of cases admitted or readmitted fell into the diagnostic category of reactive depression. Only 12% were given the diagnosis of manic-depressive psychoses; while the remaining 6% were allocated to the category of depressive neurosis. In two unpublished studies (Freeman, 1974; 1984b) the author found that approximately only 30% of admissions were diagnosed as suffering from functional psychoses and organic mental states. The remainder were diagnosed as cases of reactive depression, adjustment reaction, personality disorder, alcoholism and neuroses.

The diagnostic categories to which these non-psychotic disorders are allocated are ill defined, and lack sound criteria by means of which each condition can be differentiated from the other and from neurosis and psychosis. It is often difficult to decide if a given case should be diagnosed as an adjustment reaction of depressive type, or reactive depression. Indeed, this large group of mental disorders presents a therapeutic challenge to the psychoanalyst in the mental hospital. (The methods and techniques employed have been described at length in both the psychiatric and psychoanalytic literature.) Over and above this, however, is the question of whether or not the results of analytic work with these non-psychotic mental disorders can lead to a refinement of diagnostic criteria. Several attempts have already been made in this direction (Rangell, 1956; Reich, 1960; Kohut, 1971; Kernberg, 1974; Freeman et al., 1984). Important as this subject is for the psychoanalyst in psychiatry it does not form a major part of this work, whose main emphasis is on the problems presented by the functional psychoses.

Chapters 6, 7, 8, 9 and 10 cover a number of clinical topics which are a part of everyday psychiatric practice. They also present a theoretical perspective, one which owes its origins to the neurologist J. Hughlings Jackson (1894). Freud found that Jackson's developmental schema accommodated his clinical observations, and also enabled him to construct his most important theoretical concepts (Stengel, 1953). Psychoses, no less than other forms of mental disorder, can be examined and evaluated in terms of that developmental theory and its later elaborations by Anna Freud (1965).

The last chapter of the book consists of an account of the psychoanalyst's contribution to the treatment of the psychoses in the contemporary climate of therapeutic procedures – both psychological and pharmacological. Perhaps psychoanalysis is on the point of regaining the place it once had in the management and treatment of the psychoses. Drug therapy has been successful in dispelling the positive symptoms (see Chapter 1), but it has failed to influence the core of the morbid process. With the aid of psychoanalytic concepts, descriptive as well as explanatory, it is possible to discover the meaning of delusional and hallucinatory phenomena. Examples of this process are given in Chapter 4, on the pre-psychotic phase of the schizo-phrenias, and also in the chapter on treatment. This understanding of the patient facilitates the establishment of a relationship between patient and doctor, patient and nurse, or patient and social worker which, in the case of the chronically ill patient, in particular, can beneficially influence the management of the condition, including the supervision of drug treatment.

In conclusion it is important to emphasize that this book is about clinical problems, and not about the reactions which follow the introduction of psychoanalytic concepts into psychiatric practice. These reactions have been written about for the past 50 years or more (Menninger, W.C., 1936; Menninger, K., 1940; Stanton and Schwartz, 1954; Freeman, Cameron and McGhie, 1958; Fischer, 1972; Lucas, 1985).

The material of the book is derived from over 35 years' experience in clinical psychiatry and psychoanalysis. This experience has led to an awareness and understanding of the problems of mental illness, and the author hopes that this awareness and understanding will be communicated to the reader.

CHAPTER 1

On transitivism and appersonation

THE PHENOMENA of transitivism and appersonation, which are the subject of this chapter, are at the heart of the different psychoanalytic theories of psychosis (see Freud, 1915c; Klein, 1932; Federn, 1953). In the following chapters many accounts will be given of psychotic patients who believed that they possessed the physical and/or mental characteristics of others, and who perceived in others aspects of their physical and/or mental being. Appersonation and transitivism, the terms used by Wernicke (1906) and Bleuler (1911) to describe the clinical manifestations, are descriptive concepts and portray the way in which the patient has come to perceive himself and others. These phenomena were later explained by psychoanalysts on the basis of a loss of 'ego boundaries' (Federn, 1953; Sperling, 1944) and 'introjection-projection' mechanisms (Klein, 1946).

The majority of reports describing the phenomena of transitivism and appersonation have been drawn from established cases of schizophrenia (Bleuler, 1911; Freeman, Cameron and McGhie, 1958). Many adolescents and young adults whose psychosis, at its onset, is characterized by a paranoid symptom complex exhibit transitivistic and appersonation phenomena at some point (see the cases of William and Edith, Chapter 2). Similar phenomena occur during a manic attack: here the patient finds his experiencing of the self and others as agreeable because it represents wishes fulfilled (primary process, Freud, 1900). When there is a paranoid symptom complex, however, as at the onset of schizophrenia or paranoid psychosis, the transitivism and appersonation may be alarming and objectionable to the patient (see the cases of Sheila and May, Chapter 2).

When a psychosis becomes chronic, as in schizophrenia and in the paranoid psychoses of middle life, transitivism and appersonation do not necessarily occur in a close temporal relationship, as they do during an acute psychotic attack. In the hebephrenic-catatonic type of chronic schizophrenia the patient is not upset by the changes in himself and others unless there is an exacerbation of the illness. For example, a 26-year-old male patient who had been ill for more than six years said, 'I saw a man in church . . . when he bolted from the church I felt a part of me was made up from his semblance.' The situation is quite different in the paranoid type of chronic schizophrenia, where the patient bitterly resents the intrusion of others into the self or the appropriation by others of parts of the self.

Classification and explanations

Bleuler's (1911) classification of transitivism and appersonation within the category of accessory (secondary) symptoms of schizophrenia has its basis in the Jacksonian theory of psychosis (Jackson, 1894). Bleuler (1911) followed Jackson (1894) in believing that the effect of the morbid process, whatever its nature, led to a loss (dissolution) of advanced mental functions, and that this loss constituted the negative symptoms of the illness. These are to be found, during acute attacks, in the loss of selective attention, of the distinction between the sign and the signified, of the capacity to discriminate the bodily and mental self from that of others, and of the connection between intention and motility. All these deficits imply a loss of the 'voluntary', allowing the expression of the positive symptoms – that is, the automatic and ego-alien modes of thought (delusions), perceiving (hallucinations) and motility (negativism, catalepsy). According to Jackson disease does not create; it sets free primitive and maladaptive modes of physical and mental activity.

Transitivism and appersonation, as in the case of other positive symptoms, are a reaction to damage to healthy mental life. They occur only when there is a loss of the capacity to discriminate between the mental representations of the self and those of others. Thus, when all schizophrenic symptoms are evaluated by means of Jacksonian concepts it is clear that positive symptoms are dependent for their expression on negative symptoms (losses). The former seemingly only predominate during acute attacks, while the latter are present as long as the illness continues. The fact that positive symptoms in established cases of schizophrenia can be relieved by chemotherapy, while the negative symptoms remain refractory to their influence, indicates that such treatments do not affect the morbid process and are thus purely symptomatic (Wing, 1985; see Chapter 12).

The theory that the dissolution of healthy mental life leads to the exposure of a primitive (infantile) phase of mental functioning, where only the rudiments of a boundary separate the self from the non-self, has much to support it. The observation of infants (Freud, A. and Burlingham, 1944) and experimental studies (Piaget, 1929; Werner, 1957) confirm the occurrence of a developmental phase involving an apparently haphazard location of sensation, affect and ideation, and a limited differentiation of self and object images. The return, in psychoses, of the phase of adualism (Piaget) is the psychological counterpart to the reappearance of the positive plantar response and the grasp reflex in cerebral disease.

Freud's theory of psychosis (1911), being based on a developmental theory of mental life, also explains transitivism and appersonation as phenomena which achieve prominence because of the dissolution (regression) of the adult personality. The normal development of relationships with others Freud envisaged as a progress from a primitive state of merging with the mother (phase of primary identification) to one where self and object representations are clearly differentiated. Thus, during early childhood the mental representation of the mother is invested with libido whose aim is the satisfaction of current wishes. Later some of this libidinal object cathexis is directed to non-instinctual aims (sublimation), resulting in a more stable, less tempestuous relationship with the mother. Wishes are now tempered to the demands of reality.

In the same paper Freud postulated that an acute psychotic attack occurs whenever relating to others can no longer be sustained on the basis of the libidinal cathexis of objects, and is founded instead on primary identification (merging of self and object). This regression from object cathexis to primary identification can be regarded as a response to an internal danger provoked by sexual arousal or object loss. The merging of self and object during the acute psychotic attack is a kind of 'repression', in that it eliminates the mental representation of the real object as a source of danger. Manic attacks following object loss are illustrative here, for in these cases the merging of self and object fulfils a wish (to have and be the loved one) and thereby denies the loss.

When transitivism and appersonation cause resentment a new situation has arisen – the phenomena are no longer due to a simple merging of self and object. Such a phase may have occurred transiently at the onset of the psychosis, but it has been transformed by the resolution of the identification into its two elements (self and object). Parts of the self are carried out (externalized) on to the external object where they remain (transitivism) while some features of the object remain in the self (appersonation). The affective accompaniments of transitivism and appersonation will therefore depend on whether a state of merging predominates or whether the merging (primary identification) has been resolved.

Appersonation and transitivism are regarded by Klein (1946) and others (Rosenfeld, 1954; Segal, 1951) as a basis for their theory of infantile mental development: in these phenomena they find a repetition of an infantile phase which Klein (1946) named the paranoid-schizoid position. It is postulated that the presence of destructive forces within the infant stimulates a series of reactions (defences) designed to protect the growing self from annihilation. Both self and object images are split so that the 'good' loving parts are separated from the 'bad' destructive parts. The 'bad' parts of the self are then pushed into the object (breast) in order to control and injure it. This defence is called projective identification: for as a protection against the destructive breast-object the infant internalizes (introjects) this 'bad' image in the hope of neutralizing its effect. Further externalization of the 'bad' object continues, which heightens the dangerous nature of the object. This process of introjection and projection continues until the phase reaches its climax and is succeeded by the depressive position.

According to Klein (1946) the predisposition to schizophrenia is established if the infant fails to pass through the paranoid-schizoid position successfully. The psychosis appears when the individual fails to meet some demand of adult life. That is, there is regression and the exposure of the paranoid-schizoid position. The withdrawal, anxiety and negativism of the schizophrenic patient are explained as resulting from projective identification: the patient behaves like the infant who has pushed the 'bad' parts of himself into the object (breast). According to this theory introjection and projection are the means whereby transitivistic phenomena and appersonations arise in acute and chronic psychoses.

Relevance of the phenomena for a theory of psychosis

Freud (1911) attributed the psychological defect in psychoses to a weakness of the libidinal tie to the object. Once the object is deprived of libidinal cathexis, links with reality are severed and the self and the environment are experienced in a disturbing way. It is also of interest that transitivism and appersonation are commonly found in the psychoses and borderline states of childhood (Des Lauriers, 1959; Fleiss, 1961; Thomas, 1966). These children, just like psychotic adults, assimilate the characteristics of others and externalize some of their own physical and mental attributes; these phenomena result from the kind of primitive identification postulated as occurring in adult patients.

The transition from identification to object cathexis can be observed during psychoanalytic treatment of the borderline states of childhood (Fraiberg, 1952). Equally, there may be a reversion from object choice to identification at certain points in the therapy. These similarities between psychotic children and certain schizophrenic adults (Freeman, 1973a; 1976) can be understood as resulting from a failure to maintain or, in the case of children, reach the libidinal cathexis of objects (Freud, A., 1965).

Freud suggests that vulnerability to psychosis may lie in the tenuous nature of an individual's ties with reality, and that this weakness, however much it owes to heredity, is also the result of adverse childhood and pubertal experience. This acquired element in predisposition must vary between patients. Indeed, it is a fact of clinical experience that young adults who present with a paranoid symptom complex, and whose affects are reminiscent of manic depression, are able, in the course of psychotherapy, to describe the details of a delusional reality and to recall childhood phantasies and memories (see Chapter 5). These reconstructions (Katan, 1950, 1959) of the patient's early life present a picture not unlike that described for children whose mental development has been hindered by psychical traumata. The significant casualty is always the evolving capacity to relate to others in a steady and satisfying manner. It is a lack reflected in the widespread inhibitions characterizing the pre-psychotic personality of so many young adult patients.

Transitivism and appersonation can be explained as a primary reaction to dissolution alone in situations where they are tolerated by the patient. They banish anxiety by removing a danger, or represent the fulfilment of agreeable wishes. When transitivism and appersonation are felt as an intrusion they can no longer be regarded as a primary response to dissolution, as the Kleinians would have it. There is in fact much to commend the view that these latter forms of transitivism and appersonation are secondary phenomena resulting from a movement in mental life, the aim of which is to replace the state of identification (merging) with the object, and to re-establish the independence of the self from the object. Unfortunately, this movement – this attempt at recovery (Freud, 1911) – has only a partial success because parts of the object are left behind in the self, and parts of the self are externalized on to the object during the process of redifferentiation. Transitivism and appersonation now cause anxiety and anger, because the renewal of the distinction between self and object revives the danger which the merging (identification) had dispelled.

Freud's theory of psychosis vividly illustrates the Jacksonian principle that damage to healthy mental or nervous functions leads to the appearance of less advanced (automatic) forms of mental or nervous activity which substitute for what has been lost. Merging based on primary identification 'fills in' (McLeod, K., personal communication, 1966) for the loss of the distinction between self and object which is essential for adult interpersonal relationships. In paranoid types of psychosis (paranoid schizophrenia, paranoid psychosis) the dissolution is arrested, and an attempt is made to restructure the boundary of the self so that a separateness from the object is gained. This leads to the 'persecutory' forms of appersonation and transitivism, the result of which is no more adaptive than the hypertonia of the musculature following the flaccidity found immediately after a cerebrovascular accident.

CHAPTER 2

Nosographic aspects of schizophrenic and paranoid psychoses

THERE HAS been disagreement amongst psychoanalysts about theories of the schizophrenias and paranoid psychoses. Freud's theory (1911, 1915b, 1915c, 1924) has been criticized on several grounds (Sullivan, 1932; Federn, 1953), and major revisions of it have been made (Klein, 1932, 1946). It has been suggested by several writers (Jacobson, 1967; London, 1973; Frosch, 1983) that these controversies about theory have arisen because insufficient attention has been given to nosography. One purpose of this and the next chapter, therefore, is to demonstrate the symptomatological variation and courses of illness which occur, in the hope that the attention of psychoanalysts will be drawn to the necessity of taking account of this clinical complexity when constructing theories of psychosis.

It was the study of the courses which may be followed by different types of psychosis which enabled Kraepelin to bring hebephrenia, catatonia and dementia paranoides within the compass of Morel's dementia praecox. Kraepelin found that these types, distinct at their onset, terminated in a similar fashion ('dementia'), notwithstanding the fact that the symptoms of each type might succeed or replace one another in the same patient during the course of the illness. By introducing the concept of systematic splitting as the mental event pathognomonic of the group of schizophrenias, Bleuler (1911) focused attention on the phenomena presenting at the onset of the

illness, and on their content. To make a diagnosis of schizophrenia, in contrast to that of dementia praecox, it was no longer
necessary to take account of the course of the illness and manner
of termination. The presence of phenomena attributable to
splitting – for example, divorce of thought from reality as in
'double book-keeping' (Bleuler, 1911) – was sufficient to
establish the diagnosis.

In spite of the widespread acceptance of the concept of the
group of schizophrenias, there has always been some dissatisfaction with splitting as the diagnostic criterion (Freud, 1911).
This dissatisfaction led some psychiatrists (Langfeldt, 1960; Ey,
1959) to advocate a narrow concept of schizophrenia which, like
dementia praecox, was based on course and termination as well
as the symptomatology at onset. Others (Henderson and
Gillespie, 1969; Retterstol, 1966) preferred to limit the range of
schizophrenia by retaining the concept of persecutory paranoia
under the title of paranoid psychosis. The presence of different
symptoms and behavioural manifestations led Hecker and
Kahlbaum to conclude that hebephrenia and catatonia were
independent clinical entities. This symptomatic variation was
acknowledged later by Kraepelin and by Bleuler in their desig-
nating these conditions as distinct types of dementia praecox/
schizophrenia.

Since Bleuler (1911) and Jung (1907) demonstrated that the
contents of delusions and hallucinations are substitutes for
phantasies, memories and thoughts, contents have mostly been
regarded as data that are potentially helpful to the
psychotherapeutic process (Fromm-Reichmann, 1939; Searles,
1963; Burnham, 1955). However, the contents of delusions and
hallucinations are also an important aspect of nosography.
Similar contents are to be found in patients both at the onset and
during the course of the illness, and this consistency of content
within different groups of patients offers a further means of
distinguishing between clinical types. For example, Freud's
(1911) theory of persecutory paranoia drew attention to the
category of patients who claim that they are persecuted by a
member of their own sex known to them prior to the attack. To

refute Freud's theory, cases where the persecution is blamed on a known person of the opposite sex were quoted (see Chapter 6). Such cases are overwhelmingly female, for only rarely does a male patient complain of the persecutor being a female, other than in the role of an accomplice. This then leaves the large number of patients who believe that their persecution is initiated and sustained by an unknown agency.

A number of psychiatrists (Leonhard, 1961; Ey, 1959; Langfeldt, 1960; Kasanin, 1933) have described cases where, at the onset, affects are a prominent element of the delusional content. Mild or extreme degrees of elation (Leonhard's anxiety-elation psychosis) accompany wish (grandiose) delusions and sometimes precede them (Ey's acute delusional psychosis). For their part, psychoanalytic writers (Katan, 1974; Rosenfeld, 1954) have drawn attention to the fact that affects such as envy and jealousy manifested during treatment have an indirect expression, by way of projection, during the acute attack at the onset of the illness. Moreover, it is possible to classify acute attacks in accordance with the most striking of these delusional contents.

As persecutory symptom complexes (delusional perception, passivity experiences – the experience of thoughts, feelings, actions being controlled by persecutors – auditory hallucinations, etc.) can occur for the first time in patients over the age of 35, most frequently in women (Forrest, 1975); and run a course which is generally towards remission and often characterized by the presence of depressive phenomena (e.g. 'melancholic' delusions), it has been considered proper to distinguish this group of conditions as a nosological entity – paranoid psychosis – and so differentiate it from the schizophrenias (Batchelor, 1964; Retterstol, 1966). Such a distinction is followed here.

Chemotherapy, in modest doses, was used in all the cases described in this chapter and the next. As the latter will illustrate, this therapy did not materially alter the course of the illness, in the absence of a complete remission of symptoms, nor prevent further acute attacks in non-remitting cases (see Chapter 12).

Acute attacks at the onset

Persecution by a known member of the same sex

The uniformity of the form and content of the delusions of patients who believe that they are persecuted by a known person of the same sex is more apparent than real. There are differences with regard to the presence or absence of wish delusions, and of the affects of envy, jealousy, hate and sexuality. The way in which the self and others are perceived varies, as does the location of hallucinations when they occur.

(a) Persecutory delusions preceded or accompanied by wish/ grandiose delusions

(i) In schizophrenic psychoses

William, a 20-year-old unmarried man, was admitted to hospital because his speech and behaviour had become disturbed: he grimaced and adopted peculiar postures. His parents reported that he had been in an unusually cheerful mood for some weeks before the acute onset of the psychosis.

In this state William's eyes darted from side to side, and he turned his head as if ready to defend himself or to attack. After a few days, however, he became calmer and was able to talk about his thoughts and feelings. He claimed he was a chosen person whose mission was to help others by protecting them from evil. He had electricity in his body which could detect homosexuals. They were evil but he could cure them; this evil, however, penetrated his body and he was now forced to have homosexual thoughts. He accused the admitting doctor of being a homosexual, and got ready to attack him physically.

Later in the attack William revealed that his older brother, who had recently become betrothed, had been annoying him. The brother, in William's opinion, was a weakling and effeminate, while women looked at him, William, admiringly. His brother envied him and wanted William out of the way so that he could inherit the family property; he also had sexual desires for their sister. Of late his brother had taken to following William everywhere and imitating his gestures, behaviour and manner of dress; he was turning into a replica of himself (transitivism). His brother was also trying to undermine his masculinity and render him effeminate and a homosexual.

Envy as an element of the delusional content: Envy is an element of the delusional content when there are wish delusions accompanying the persecutory ideas. James, aged 20, was referred for a psychiatric opinion when he became fearful and aggressive. He told his parents that there were men in the garden of the house waiting to kill him; he heard their voices repeating his own thoughts and referring to incidents in his life which no one could know. His hands had moved without any intention on his part to carry out an act.

Until two weeks before he had been off work owing to an eye injury; he had been attacked by several youths, and only his proficiency in judo had saved him. After being in this new employment for a few weeks he noticed that one of the female employees was interested in him. Someone had told him that she had an illegitimate child, and he concluded that she had fallen in love with him. Her father would give him £100,000 when he married her. (The patient's father had been worried about his son at this time because he was unusually elated and excited.) James said later that when he was walking in the street people looked at him admiringly – 'I was as well known as the Lord Mayor.'

Some days before the appearance of the persecutory fears a male colleague asked James to join him for lunch, and at the restaurant James noticed two men sitting at a nearby table. He thought that they must be relatives of the woman who had come to look him over, which gave him an uneasy feeling. It occurred to him that the colleague had asked him to lunch so that these relatives could listen in to the conversation; later that day he concluded that the colleague was a spy posted to keep him under surveillance. Then over the next days his fears increased. Now he believed that the woman in the office had only pretended to be in love with him in order to lure him into a trap. She would lead him to the men with whom he had had the fight, and they would kill him. Next he refused to leave the house and walked about with an antique sword in his hand. He was also afraid to sleep, in case he might be attacked in the night, and on the night before being seen by the author he slept with his father. The persecutory fears subsided, only to be replaced by the fear that his father intended to kill him – drug him and then drown him. James said that his father was envious of his strength and prowess at athletics and judo: 'I am as strong as a bull and as light as a feather,' he said.

In female patients envy may be given as the reason for another woman's hostility. An adolescent girl, Edith, refused to go to school, giving as her reason that the other girls and the teachers said she smelled. No other positive symptoms appeared until she complained to her mother one day that a boy was watching her through a telescope while she undressed for bed or a bath. Other boys were standing outside the house shouting that she was 'a good thing' (i.e. promiscuous). Edith became restless, rushing out of the house, walking up and down the street talking to strangers, entering neighbours' houses uninvited. When mother and sister tried to restrain her Edith attacked them, attempting to stab her mother with a knife, claiming that the mother was a witch. Edith then attacked her favourite sister, accusing her of envying her feminine charms. She shouted at the sister: 'You want to be me because I am better looking than you, that is why I am on TV.' But prior to this attack she had cut her hair in an attempt to fashion it in the same style as that of her sister, and then used her sister's cosmetics and head scarf (appersonation).

Edith was admitted to mental hospital much against her will, and tried in every way she could to leave the ward. She tore off her nightdress and darted about the ward naked, exposed her genitalia and masturbated, and was incontinent of urine. She would admire her unclothed body in front of a mirror, and would feel her breasts and buttocks, saying 'I love my body.' When a slightly built nurse approached her she ran at her threateningly and said, 'You hate me because you want to be me. You are making me flat chested, you envy me, you are making me like you.'

Jealousy as an element of the delusional content: There are patients whose psychosis begins with wish/grandiose delusions and where jealousy is believed by the patients to be the cause of the known persecutor's behaviour. Mary, a young woman of 18, claimed that God had entrusted her with the mission of 'saving' her cousin. Mary had not seen this cousin for two years or more, and feared for his soul. On admission to hospital she was overactive and excited, striking out at the nurses because they were stopping her from seeing her cousin, who she believed was also a patient in the hospital (transitivism). During the excited phase she announced that she was God; later that the cousin was in love with her (erotomania), and that he had left because she had not responded to him. Now his mother would not tell her where he was because she was jealous. His mother was spreading rumours to the effect that she was promiscuous, had been pregnant but had undergone an abortion.

Sexual content as an element of the delusional complex: During acute attacks it is commonplace to encounter anxieties about heterosexuality and homosexuality (see the cases of William, Sheila, Nan, Tom and Richard). There are patients who claim that a member of their own sex is imposing homosexual wishes and thoughts on them (see the cases of William and Tom) against their will (passivity experiences). In other cases it is heterosexual sensations or ideas which are induced by the persecutor.

There is yet another group of patients who complain that the persecutor is spreading a rumour that they are homosexual, or that they are heterosexually promiscuous and oversexed. In these patients passivity experiences are absent. Take the case of Peter, a university student aged 20, who believed that a fellow student was spreading a rumour that he was a homosexual. Peter was being accused of having had a sexual relationship with the curator of the science museum in his home town, a 50-year-old man who had taken an interest in the patient's career. The rumour had started with a poem which had been published in the student magazine; Peter claimed that there was a hidden reference to his being a homosexual.

In his first term at university Peter found himself attracted to a girl student, but he was shy and ill at ease in her company, feeling that his knowledge of sexual matters was inadequate and therefore must be inferior to hers as she was a biology student. He had the impulse to change his course to biology, and decided to join a student society, the Sexual Reform Society, in the hope that he might get advice on how to approach the girl and initiate a relationship. When Peter first met the girl he thought she must be the daughter of a lecturer whom she resembled facially. He found notes in lecture theatres and in the library suggesting that he was effeminate.

These persecutory ideas were accompanied by wish delusions. In the second term of his first year Peter claimed that he had designed original pieces of scientific equipment; he was about to write a paper which would demolish a theory advanced by a distinguished research worker. This Peter was going to do because the man was an evil influence, and if his views were accepted mankind would suffer. A great poet would make him, Peter, famous by referring to him as an outstanding scientist. But this thought had frightened him because his name had now been besmirched, and instead of being acclaimed he would be despised.

(ii) In paranoid psychoses
Envy as an element of the delusional content: A married farmer, Charles, aged 42, complained of being hypnotized by terrorists and forced to carry out acts of violence. Fearful for his brother, who worked for a government agency, he believed that the terrorists had singled him out because of his brilliant intellect, 'a brain like a computer'. These delusional ideas rapidly receded with chemotherapy, however.

During the next five years Charles remained tolerably well after a period of low spirits and lethargy. A further acute attack ensued, and once again he believed that because of his outstanding abilities he was being used by terrorists. After a short remission he fell ill again, this time claiming that his wife was trying to poison him. She was mentally ill, he claimed (transitivism), and was being forced to poison him by his elder brother. The brother had told Charles's wife that if she did not do as he said he would tell Charles that his wife had had an illegitimate child before they married (Charles and his wife were childless). Charles had discovered this plot through brilliant detective work, and was convinced that his brother wanted him dead because he was envious, and wanted the farm for himself. After some months, as before, these delusional ideas disappeared.

Jealousy as an element of the delusional content: The patient, Sheila, was a married woman of 32. She reported that a colleague at work, a 54-year-old widow with whom she had been friendly, was spreading malicious tales about her. Sheila had trusted this woman, who had confided in her. Now, however, the woman was maligning Sheila, saying she was promiscuous, and in particular alleging that Sheila had designs on a senior colleague. Then one day the patient heard this man say to others that she 'had stripped him with her eyes'. At first she thought he must be joking, but then realized that he was serious: clearly he had believed that she had wanted to touch his penis. After this the older woman became more and more outrageous in her accusations, and would say to the men in the office, 'You like her because she is like that.' Sheila concluded that the widow behaved in this way because *she was jealous of the attentions* the senior colleague had paid to her younger friend.

Soon after, Sheila heard announcers on the television and radio say 'She's like that, you know,' and felt she was being treated like a criminal. At the same time, unpleasant thoughts of a sexual and sadistic kind forced themselves into her mind – 'I don't want to think about them . . . I was never like that . . . when I see a man I think he has an erection and it is the same with women.' While in hospital she also said that other patients were using her voice to criticize her (transitivism), and reported that she had had the phantasy, while sitting talking to a woman doctor, of sticking a knife into the doctor. The phantasy was accompanied by an exciting, vicious feeling, and Sheila was immediately distressed and agitated.

(b) Persecutory delusions preceded by erotomania
(i) In schizophrenic psychoses
The persecution which may follow erotomania is frequently attributed to a known person of the same sex. For example, Emma, a single woman of 19, fell ill while at university. Emma lived at home with her parents, and complained that she was being pestered by a young man who had been in her class at university; actually she hardly knew him. The young man was in love with her, but for some unknown reason was sending messages through the television and radio, claiming that they had been sexually intimate, but angry with her for not agreeing to coitus. In spite of this, Emma knew he loved her. If he did not present himself to her in person it was because his mother objected to the relationship – she was *jealous* of Emma. His mother was humiliating her in different ways: for instance, sitting in a restaurant with her parents, Emma heard his mother say, 'Take off your pants.' Emma believed that everyone in the restaurant had heard this and she rushed out in a state of embarrassment.

The jealousy expressed in the delusional content is frequently found in cases where erotomania is followed by persecution by a known person of the same sex. This was to be observed in the following case of paranoid psychosis.

(ii) In paranoid psychoses
The patient, Nan, a single woman of 30, was referred for psychotherapy on account of a depression which did not respond to anti-depressant medications. Only later did she disclose that some years earlier a university lecturer had been in love with her; this led to a spell in mental hospital.

The depressive state was treated by group psychotherapy. Nan attended the weekly meetings regularly and appeared to benefit, but it became obvious that she idealized the author who conducted the group. Nan worried lest she prove a burden or a nuisance, and was concerned about his health. Two and a half years after starting therapy, which enabled her to lead a normal life, both socially and professionally, she told the group that a man was in love with her, adding that she was angry with her landlady because the woman was interfering in her affairs.

A short time later Nan asked to see the author alone, and told him that she knew he was in love with her. She claimed, erroneously, that he had found work for her and looked after her interests and safety. Further, she had seen him walking outside the school where she taught, and from the window of her flat. A week later Nan appeared at the group in distress, and announced that she was the victim of a plot organized by the author's wife, who had secretly installed a television camera in Nan's bedroom so that she could record love-making between Nan and her husband. Indeed, the night before, Nan had been aware of the author's body in her bed; he was being victimized, like herself (transitivism). He could not declare his love because of *his wife's jealousy*. The author's wife was trying to ruin her reputation by telling everyone that Nan masturbated and thought of nothing but men. The delusion continued for several months; it was replaced by low spirits, loss of energy and interest in life.

(c) Persecutory delusions alone
(i) In schizophrenic psychoses
In many cases of schizophrenia the delusional content at the onset consists solely of persecutory phenomena. For example, Tom, a 19-year-old, said that he was being victimized by a fellow student. Shortly after Tom went into hospital he attacked a male nurse, claiming that the nurse had winked at him, insinuating that they might have a homosexual relationship.

For several weeks Tom had noticed that the behaviour of the fellow student, with whom he had been friendly, had changed. The student now appeared to be watching him and seemed critical. Tom came to suspect that the student had been instructed to keep him under surveillance, a suspicion that was reinforced when Tom discovered that the contents of his locker were not in their usual place. Then when his experiments in the science laboratory went inexplicably wrong he became convinced that his friend wanted to do him harm by interfering in his affairs. He noticed that persons in the street winked at him;

his brother had done so too and this angered him.

These symptoms disappeared after a period of hospitalization, and Tom returned home. Some months later, however, there was a relapse, following shortly after an evening out with a girl who was his sister's friend. Tom retired to bed and refused to get up. A day later his mother noticed some blood on his pillow, saw some superficial cuts on his throat and called the doctor, who arranged for his admission to hospital. On this occasion the persecutory fears were absent, and instead there was a wish delusion, the content of which consisted of thoughts about the girl mentioned above. Tom had known her only slightly, and had not mentioned her during the first attack. A day or so after taking the girl to the theatre Tom saw her and gave her a poem he had written; he also said, 'I love you.' The girl was taken aback and told him not to be silly. The suicidal attack was a reaction to this event, and Tom later said: 'My mind was unbalanced when I did it, it was to make someone very sorry.'

It was during this latter phase of the illness that information came to hand about Tom's close relationship with his older brother, who was of an independent and active nature. Tom always followed his lead and based his own opinions, attitudes and behaviour on those of the brother. This had been so from the time that they were both at boarding school, with the older brother acting as protector and guide. After school days Tom spent a great deal of time in his brother's company, but the close relationship was disrupted when the brother became seriously involved with a girl. To this time Tom had shown no interest in girls on his own account, and when the brother's girlfriend visited the family home Tom was noticeably withdrawn and unenthusiastic, regarding her as an intruder. While he did not admit to jealousy, his attitude and behaviour admitted to no other explanation. Indeed, this psychotic attack occurred not long after the brother's announcement of his engagement to the girl.

(ii) In paranoid psychoses
Persecutory phenomena frequently comprise the sole content of

delusions at the onset of a paranoid psychosis. Richard, a single man of 38, said that a former male friend was spreading a rumour to the effect that he was having affairs with married women. Richard had known the persecutor for a long time, and in recent months had been meeting him frequently at a religious group. Richard also believed that his house was 'bugged' by the police at the instigation of the former friend. It had crossed his mind that the reason for the persecution might be that years ago he had been sexually attracted to the persecutor's wife and that the man had found out: clearly the husband *was jealous* and wanted revenge.

Persecution by a known member of the opposite sex

Delusions of persecution by members of the opposite sex in schizophrenic and paranoid psychoses are predominantly, if not entirely, found in women. If a woman is part of a man's persecutory delusion he spontaneously reveals that she is merely an instrument or an accomplice of the male persecutor (as in the case of Charles). The male persecutor is known to the patient: he may be her former lover, friend or acquaintance; or her doctor, dentist or a man with whom she has had no real contact.

(a) Persecution preceded by erotomania

(i) In schizophrenic psychoses
May, an unmarried woman of 24 years of age, complained that a man whom she believed to have loved her was reading her mind and causing her great mental and physical distress. She had attended him for some years in his professional capacity as a dentist, but otherwise had no contact with him. She would daydream about his love for her, enjoying erotic phantasies. The man was about 40 years old and unmarried, and according to May the persecution began shortly after a friend told her that there was a suspicion that the man was a homosexual. She began to hear his voice in her head: what he said was critical of her, often of a sexual nature. After her admission to hospital May said that she was being forced by him to experience everything that he experienced, to feel and act as he did. She also claimed

that she had to endure clitoral sensations every time he masturbated. The man was mentally ill (transitivism) and a patient in
the hospital; he was corrupting her by causing her to masturbate,
and he was trying to make her into a homosexual.

Jealousy and envy as elements of the delusional content: Where
erotomania is followed by persecution by a known member of
the same sex, the patient attributes the malevolent behaviour of
her persecutor to jealousy (see the case of Nan). By the same
token, since a third party is not present in the delusional complex
where erotomania is followed by persecution by a man, there can
be no question of jealousy. However, evidence of envy can
sometimes be observed, as in the instance of Rachael, a married
woman who had suffered from two psychotic attacks, one at the
age of 19 and a second at the age of 26. She fell ill again when she
was 31 years of age.

Rachael complained that a former boyfriend stood outside her
house every night in a state of sexual excitement, shouting insults
at her. This man had in fact kept company with her for three
years, when Rachael had been 16 to 18 years old, and then ended
the relationship. Her first attack followed this disappointment,
and during it she believed that he must be mentally ill (transitivism) to act as he did. He wanted revenge because he believed
her to be responsible for the fact that his second child was
mentally defective; he envied her because she had healthy
children. Thus, psychotherapeutic work with female patients
who believe that they are persecuted by a man suggests that
hatred of the persecutor is in part derived from envy (Katan,
1974).

(ii) Persecutory delusions alone
Women who complain, at the onset of the illness, that they are
persecuted by a man fall into two groups: those who had a real
love relationship with the man prior to the psychotic attack, and
those who had no real knowledge of the male persecutor. An
example of the former group is Clare, a young nurse aged 19,
who suddenly fell ill, becoming restless, anxious and at times
euphoric. She said that colleagues believed her to be a prosti-

tute, and on admission to hospital expressed doubts about her sexual identity, asking 'Am I a woman?' Clare thought the women patients were men dressed as women, and complained of dimness of vision, and of having a squint. She also believed that she was being hypnotized by her former lover and forced to experience sexual ideas and feelings. She then accused him of making her behave like a prostitute.

According to her mother, Clare had been in low spirits during the two months prior to the attack, and had lost interest in her work, her mother attributing this change to a disappointment in love. Clare had in fact been keeping company with a young man for almost a year. She met him initially while nursing in the ophthalmic ward of the hospital, to which he had been admitted for the treatment of a squint. During her stay in mental hospital Clare revealed that she had had regular coitus with him, which she had done out of love for him, and because he promised to marry her.

In the case of the second group, the persecutor, although a real person, is one with whom the patient has had no contact in reality. Kath, for example, a young woman aged 20, became withdrawn and reluctant to join in company. One night she burst into tears, shouting 'I hate him, I hate him.' A young man whom she had met only once a year previously, and had not seen since, was making her life a misery: she could hear his voice outside in the street and he would not go away. He was also spreading nasty stories about her. When seen by a psychiatrist Kath complained of a difficulty in making connections between phrases and sentences, and sometimes she could hear her own voice arguing with her. Gradually a negativism came to characterize her behaviour: she was easily aroused to anger, refused to talk to anyone, denied her parentage and would curse her mother and father if they came to the hospital. Catatonic signs developed.

(b) In paranoid psychoses
It is not uncommon to encounter women in the age range of 40 to 60 who complain of being persecuted by a man, often a doctor or dentist. For instance, a patient of 50 years of age had a hysterec-

tomy. A few months later she developed the false idea that the surgeon was telling lies about her, to the effect that she was promiscuous and had VD; she heard it, she said, on TV and radio.

Persecution by unknown persons or agencies

(a) Persecutory delusions preceded or accompanied by wish/ grandiose delusions
(i) In schizophrenic psychoses
Robert, a young man of 21, complained that his every thought and action was controlled by a computer (an influencing machine), but he could not discover where the computer was located. He had looked everywhere to find it and to discover the name of the scientist who had constructed it. For Robert believed that he had made scientific discoveries in the same field of electronics, but that there was a movement afoot to stop him getting the credit for his genius. The computer was introducing ideas into his mind which were foreign to his normal way of thinking: he found himself speaking when he did not mean to, and the words he uttered were not his own. Then he had to endure headaches, pains in the limbs and difficulties with vision when the computer was activated. Unable to understand why all this was happening to him, Robert wondered if the scientist persecuting him was envious of his creative ability.

(ii) In paranoid psychoses
Derek, an unmarried man of 38, believed that Christ was returning to earth in the guise of an astronaut to save the world; Christ was accompanied by a group of spacemen from another planet. Derek believed himself to be a part of this project and was elated by the idea, and he also believed that he was married to a woman he had long admired but did not know personally. Some weeks later, however, he began to fear that the astronauts were hostile rather than friendly, and his mind and body seemed to be possessed by an alien being. Thus he found his eyes focusing on signs which suggested his imminent death. A loss of morning erections he attributed to the persecutors (the

astronauts), fearing that the penile sensations heralded gangrene of that organ.

Derek supported his claim that he was possessed by pointing to what he believed to be crescent-shaped marks on his arms and legs. The crescent, he said, was the insignia of the astronauts, and its presence on his body indicated that he was being transformed into one of them (appersonation). He was to carry out, on their instructions, their destructive and nefarious plans. Had he been responsible for acts of murder, violence and rape? Derek's agitated state indicated that he believed he had already committed unpardonable crimes.

(b) Persecutory delusions alone
(i) In schizophrenic psychoses

Harry, a young man of 19, feared that he was having a bad effect on others, and was acutely anxious. 'If I look in your eyes, you will be heartbroken,' he said to the author. 'I am betraying you,' he added. At the same time he believed that he was under surveillance, and he feared a murderous attack on himself, which would be launched by a creature he called a paranoidal. This was half man and half woman and lived by preying on humans, and it had the power to direct Harry's attention to ideas of a destructive kind. Harry perceived himself and others as both bodily and mentally altered – 'Am I a man or a woman, or both?' was his question, and he thought he was being turned into a woman.

(ii) In paranoid psychoses

Joan, an unmarried woman aged 40, complained that unknown persecutors were causing her to experience the bodily sensations of others, the most distressing of which were those in the genital area. For instance, Joan had to endure the frustration of a man whose penis was being interminably stimulated by a woman, without orgasm. At other times the experience was that of a woman being sexually stimulated by a man. Because Joan had been turned by the persecutors into a composite person, made up of different individuals (appersonation), a pain in her head was the headache of someone else. If a woman was in labour, Joan experienced her labour pains.

Envy as an element of the delusional complex: In cases where the persecutor is unknown it is not uncommon for the patient to attribute the persecution to envy (see the case of Robert), in these cases jealousy cannot be a cause of the persecution. Sometimes the persecutory attack is preceded or followed by one or more bouts of depression characterised by self-reproaches (see the case of Don, p. 47).

Acute attacks in schizophrenias which have terminated in 'moderate' or 'moderately severe end states'

Acute attacks of brief duration are commonplace in cases of schizophrenia which have terminated in 'moderate', 'moderately severe' or 'severe end states' (Bleuler, M., 1978). The delusional and hallucinatory phenomena characteristic of these acute attacks have a predominantly persecutory character, but the content may also be of a grandiose/wish-fulfilling nature, as in the following case.

Persecution by a known member of the same sex

In the case of Tom, termination was in a severe end state. His speech was difficult to follow because of derailment of thought and by the formation of neologism; he had lost interest in his appearance, and looked unkempt and neglected. There was active as well as passive negativism (Bleuler, 1911). The wish delusions, which appeared soon after the onset of the psychosis, took the form, as mentioned above, of a belief that the girl to whom he had given the poem loved him and was waiting to marry him. The marriage would take place whenever he was awarded a pension for reconstructing the hospital, which, according to his delusional thinking, had been destroyed shortly before his admission.

Despite this state of chronicity, an attempt was made to make contact with Tom through daily meetings. But after some months, during which he revealed his wish delusions, the relationship with the author began to deteriorate. Tom was disappointed because the latter had failed to procure the pension for him, and he became depressed in mood – 'I'm a most unfortunate person, all my work is taken for granted.' He complained that his face, of which he was very proud, was being altered in shape and the texture of the skin changed. The author was accused of causing this through electrical waves coming from the TV. In general Tom was threatening in manner, and domineering.

Another case is that of Henry, a single man of 28 who had been ill for eight years. In quiescent phases Henry was withdrawn and neglectful of himself, but during an acute attack he said that his father was an animal – crude, cunning and deceitful. His father had committed murder but the police could not find the bodies or give evidence against him. His father *envied* him because he was a genius: he had invented scientific instruments but his father had stolen the plans and had sold them. His father had successfully convinced everyone that he, Henry, was insane.

At the onset of the psychosis Henry asserted that someone was trying to make him homosexual, and that he was being forced to wish to have coitus per anum with a man. During the acute attack referred to here he spoke as follows to the author – 'Your shoes are well polished.' When the author said that Henry was very observant, he continued, 'I'm not queer, I do not think you are either. Did you know I was raped some while ago? A fellow gave me bad whiskey when I was out for a drink. The next thing I knew I was being raped.' The man penetrated his anus, he reported – 'It was like a shotgun going off.' After this boys in the street called him a queer and accused him of wanting to have sexual relations with them.

Persecution by a known member of the opposite sex

Periodic attacks characterized by the delusion of being persecuted by a man are found in long-standing female cases of schizophrenia. Hilda fell ill at the age of 14, saying that men were looking at her when she was bathing or undressing for bed. She accused her father of raping her, and attacked him with a knife. From time to time she would become disturbed, saying that her father was interfering with her thoughts. He wanted to corrupt her and then have her destroyed. The illness proceeded to a severe end state.

Persecution by unknown persons or agencies

The repetition of elements of the content of the first psychotic attack during the chronic phase of the illness (severe end state) is illustrated by the case of Ann, a 35-year-old patient. Ann fell ill initially at the age of 13, when the first sign of mental disturbance was an unwillingness to go to school. At this time her mother was pregnant, and Ann did not want to leave her side in case she, the mother, might die. (There was also an older sister and an older brother.) At school Ann's concentration was poor and she was forgetful; the teachers complained that she forgot her school books and pens, while at home she was forever mislaying things. She was withdrawn from school on the advice of the doctor and remained at home until the baby, a boy, was born. Now in her fourteenth year Ann returned to school but her performance was, if anything, worse – she was reported as withdrawn and uninterested, and sometimes her responses were nonsensical or incomprehensible. After a bout of 'uninhibited' behaviour at home hospitalization was recommended. It was at this time that she claimed that she was pregnant.

Ann remained in hospital for six months. During this time her mental state oscillated between bouts of excitement and periods of withdrawal and negativistic behaviour. In an excited phase she said that a man, possibly a pop star, was in love with her: she knew that he wanted to come and see her but he was prevented by her sister and mother, who *were jealous*. She masturbated openly and when asked about it replied that a man was making her do it. However, her condition improved somewhat with chemotherapy, and she returned home. The further course of the illness was characterized by a pronounced volitional 'defect', speech disorder and neglect of herself, and in spite of continuing medication there were frequent acute attacks.

The patient lived for long periods with her mother, who had been widowed when Ann was 23 years old. Ann was periodically admitted to hospital on account of these acute attacks, which might last for several months. The following utterances occurred during an attack when she was 33 years old – 'My father is not a rich man, he is not my father, I have a son by him, he was born when I was 14 years old [her age at the birth of her brother], I just heard that fact.' After a pause she continued: 'He is not my son, I am not his daughter at all. She [the mother] had to get married to him, she is very bossy, tells me to brush my teeth and wash my hair. My son is doing his job at the university [brother was at university, aged 19]. She thought he was her son. It was explained to her, what else could he be but my son?' A further pause was followed by 'He is not my son at all, he is the woman [i.e. the mother] in the house's son ['double book-keeping', Bleuler, 1911]. She is not my mother, I do not believe I have a brother or sister or anything. My real mother comes from an aristocratic family. My dad is a proper prince.'

Ann's jealousy and hate of the baby brother, born, as mentioned, when she was 14 years old, were expressed most poignantly, in this acute attack, in the following utterance: 'The only way the baby could be saved was by taking my life.' Her life had indeed ended with the birth of the brother. During this acute attack, characterized by passivity experiences, mostly of a sexual kind, she constantly referred to her jealousy or to the jealousy of others. For example: 'I was very jealous of my sister getting married, every time I wanted a husband someone interfered.' 'I am very jealous because she [the mother] looked after my sister before looking after me.' 'My younger brother is very jealous of me.'

CHAPTER 3

Nosography and the course of schizophrenic and paranoid psychoses

THE PURPOSE of the last chapter was to illustrate the variation in content which occurs between and within delusional complexes which are common to numbers of patients. That is, there is a diversity as well as a uniformity of clinical phenomena. The distinctive nature of certain delusional contents occurring at onset offers a means of classification. These distinctive contents are to be found independently of the age of the patient at the onset of the illness, of the associated clinical manifestations (hebephrenic, catatonic) or of the course of the illness.

Persecution by a known member of the same sex

(a) Persecutory delusions preceded or accompanied by wish delusions
(i) In schizophrenic psychoses
The course of illness which occurred in the case of Mary, described in the last chapter (p. 20), is illustrative of one of the outcomes of illness in patients who present initially with a combination of wish and persecutory delusions. In this case a number of acute psychotic attacks occurred over a sixteen-year period. Between attacks Mary was able to work and enjoy a limited social life; she periodically fell in love but never had any real heterosexual relationships. During acute attacks delusional contents were of a sexual nature, causing anxiety and distress. They were the work of those who hated her, she said, and wished

to deprive her of the happiness she knew lay in the love of her cousin (erotomania). During one acute épisode, for instance, Mary heard the front door of her house close and a car in the street move off. She was sure that her cousin had come to see her but, on the instructions of his mother, her parents had told him to leave. Then a female neighbour had told everyone that she had been in hospital to have an abortion. (She had, in fact, spent two days in hospital; to have a mole removed.) Bouts of depression were commonplace during the quiescent (non-delusional) periods.

In a number of cases presenting with a combination of wish and persecutory delusions the illness follows a cyclical course without serious damage to the personality. In the case of William, for instance, the first attack subsided after three months. Following the loss of the positive symptoms, a depressive affect appeared, and this fluctuated in intensity. He was able to work and continue a reasonably normal life, but further attack with a similar delusional content occurred after eight months. Once again a remission of the positive symptoms took place, and William returned home and to work. Over the next eight years there was a cycle of acute attacks with identical content and remission without any evidence of personality deterioration.

The course of the illness may be to complete recovery, as in the case of Peter (see Chapter 2). Peter remained well and without relapse in the seven years after the beginning of the illness – but although he prospered in his work he remained unmarried and unattached. A further instance of a similar outcome is that of Edward, a young man aged 18, who had not been able to leave his house for eighteen months. Edward believed that men looked at him because his face was girlish; they were excited by his appearance, just as he was when masturbating and thinking about a girl. He did not wash, so that if a man saw him he would be disgusted rather than excited by his appearance. Edward also misinterpreted actions by doctors and nurses as indicating their belief that he was a homosexual. Like Peter, too, he claimed that he had made important scientific discoveries. Gradually the delusional ideas receded, and five years later Edward had not had a recurrence of them, but he led a solitary life and worked as a labourer. In another case, that of James, a course to almost complete recovery occurred.

(ii) In paranoid psychoses
The course of illness in cases of paranoid psychosis where wish delusions accompany the delusion of being persecuted by a known member of the same sex is usually towards remission with complete recovery or a recurrence of attacks. Elsie, a married woman aged 45, accused a woman neighbour, with whom she had previously been very friendly, of causing her to be subjected to humiliating sexual experiences and of corrupting her sons; as a reprisal Elsie had thrown a stone at the neighbour's house and smashed a window. Elsie also believed that the neighbour had secretly administered a substance to her which made her receptive to the sexual advances of men, and she was critical of her husband because he did nothing to stop the persecution. She thought that he was possibly in league with her persecutor. Elsie's husband could not give an exact date of the onset of the symptoms, however, and thought that they had been present for about a year.

For her part, Elsie did not acknowledge that she was mentally ill, and she had difficulty distinguishing her own sensations, affects and thoughts from those of others who were emotionally significant for her. In this connection she said, 'I've discovered I have the power to take over bodies and voices. I take them into myself and my voice can change and I talk with their voice. My niece in Australia, she is about 20, I've taken her body lots of times, I can look at her and she becomes part of me. The last time she was home I thought she could read my mind.'

This tendency to assimilate external objects into the self (appersonation) was also to be observed in the case of the important men with whom Elsie had coitus in phantasy (the men were imposed on her by the persecutor). She said: 'Mr C [a leading political figure] came to me and was part of me after that, I was the government.' At times she had doubts about her identity, particularly if taken up with a pleasing phantasy which gave expression to her masculine wishes – 'I've been wondering lately who I am, I think I'm next to God, of course I do not know who God is, I could be Sister D or Dr W [a man].'

During this acute phase of the psychosis Elsie frequently referred to the subject of homosexuality – 'I know a lot of things are to do with homosexuals. I saw a film on TV, a very arty thing about homosexuals, and one of the men in the film screamed when he was shot. My son who was in the bathroom screamed at the same time, I thought it was because he was a homosexual too. I told my husband and my neighbour [the persecutor] that if they interfered with him I would kill them. I believe my husband has been a homosexual.'

An instance of a cyclical course is provided by the case of Charles. In the case of Sheila there was a movement towards chronicity. Hallucinatory voices with a persecutory content replaced the original delusions (see Chapter 6).

(b) Persecutory delusions (by same sex) preceded by erotomania
(i) In schizophrenic psychoses
Emma is illustrative of this type of case, in that her erotomania was followed by persecution by a known woman – the mother of the 'beloved'. Acute attacks characterized by delusional and hallucinatory experiences occurred during the first three years of the illness. These attacks gradually diminished in frequency, allowing Emma to undertake clerical work in a sheltered environment. Her level of efficiency fluctuated, however, occurring when there was a recurrence of delusional ideas. Eight years after onset the condition fell into the category of 'moderate end state'.

In other cases the outcome may be less favourable, with the illness terminating in a 'moderately severe' to 'severe end state'. For example, Christine, an unmarried woman of 23, became seriously depressed after a man, with whom she actually had expectations of marriage, gave her up. The depression lasted for six months, after which she remained well for two years. She became transiently depressed again a year prior to the onset of the acute psychotic attack, the first sign of which was Christine's announcement that her former lover had been trying to contact her at her place of work. He had now realized that he loved her and could not live without her. Christine was taken for a holiday but at the hotel waited constantly for the former lover to appear, claiming that he was in the hotel but was not allowed to see her.

Christine's preoccupation with the delusion was accompanied by an inability to concentrate on her work. She was admitted to hospital, where she remained for some months; however, no real change for the better occurred. Within weeks of coming home the withdrawal increased with negativism and hallucinatory phenomena – 'I can hear his voice,' she said. She also accused a female cousin who was brought to look after her of stopping her from seeing her beloved; the cousin was jealous, she said. Christine was then readmitted to hospital, and after a few months made an attachment to a male (hospital) doctor. This man took the place of the fiancé, and remained so even when he had left the hospital. Christine claimed that the cousin, because she was jealous, had enlisted the support of the former fiancé to stop her seeing her beloved doctor. The cousin was interfering with her thoughts and trying to drive her mad. This delusion continued unaltered for thirty years, leading to alternating bouts of negativism and aggressiveness, and as a result Christine had to be confined to hospital.

(ii) In paranoid psychoses
No case available.

(c) Persecutory delusions alone
(i) In schizophrenic psychoses
Where, at onset, there are persecutory delusions alone (persecution by a known member of the same sex), the course of the illness is one towards a moderately severe or severe end state. In the case of Tom, the relapse following the first remission brought with it a new delusional complex, which took the place of the dread of being thought to be a homosexual; the new content concerned the girl who, Tom believed, had humiliated him in the

street. He announced that she was in love with him, and the following is a verbatim report of how he experienced the delusional love relationship:

> I hardly met her in five years, only two or three times. She stayed away because she loved me and because of the imperfections of the world. I have searched every woman of the world and she is the most beautiful. There is nothing good enough for me but a woman untouched by human hand. I have sustained her spirit. Why should God not give me a creature equal to myself and similar to me? She will send everyone away and only want peace with one man.

Tom's psychosis progressed inexorably, without remission. He lost interest in his appearance, as mentioned, and became increasingly withdrawn and negativistic; his speech became difficult to follow because of derailment of thought and the formation of neologisms. Moreover, ten years later Tom was still expressing his love delusion, and was grandiose, overvaluing his physical and intellectual powers. As reported in the last chapter, however, this grandiosity was periodically disturbed by the acute anxiety caused by another of his beliefs, that his body suffered from the actions of persecutors.

A similar onset and course of illness occurred in the case of Kath.

(ii) In paranoid psychoses
Geraldine, a married woman aged 33, complained that a neighbour who lived behind her had begun insulting her, and had not only turned all her friends against her, but was influencing her children against her. Sometimes Geraldine heard her neighbour's voice on the television and radio. This persecutory symptom complex continued for about five years in spite of medications. It then disappeared, to be followed by a depressive symptomatology, and after a further two years there was no recurrence of the persecutory manifestations.

As mentioned above, the appearance of depressive manifesta-

tions during the course of a psychosis characterized by a persecutory symptom complex is by no means uncommon.

Persecution by a known member of the opposite sex

*(a) Persecutory delusions preceded or accompanied by wish
delusions*
(i) In schizophrenic psychoses
Fiona, a young woman of 26, had fallen ill a year after her
father's death when she was 20 years of age. She said that her
unmarried brother, whose bedroom was next to hers, was
putting thoughts into her head while she was asleep. He had
come into the room in the night and raped her, and did it because
he hated her. She then decided to sleep downstairs, but one night
heard footsteps on the stairs, and thought her brother was
coming to kill her; she ran out of the house in a panic. On
admission to hospital Fiona said that after reading a verse in the
Bible she had realized that she had actually spoken to Prince
Charles and that they were to marry: God had chosen her for this
mission. She also insisted that her mother was not her mother;
her real mother, she believed, was a doctor's wife who had lived
nearby when she was a child.

After some months these delusional ideas disappeared. No
more was seen of Fiona as she did not attend for out-patient
appointments, but five years later she was readmitted to
hospital. There was no deterioration in her speech, and her
appearance showed that there was no self-neglect, but there had
been unusual behaviour and threats of suicide. Fiona was now
unemployed and living at home with her mother. She had gone
into several shops and, in full view of the assistants, had taken
several items without paying. She also said that everyone,
including herself, was under the control of the Russian leader
Brezhnev: he made her curse, shout and threaten her mother.
She found that her tongue and lips formed words automatically;
there was no actual voice in her head, but someone was using her
tongue to speak thoughts which were not her own. These
thoughts could be critical, friendly, advising, etc., and everyone
was affected this way (transitivism). People talked to each other

without realizing they were doing so.

Fiona was no longer concerned with her brother, nor did she believe that she was to marry Prince Charles. She was concerned with the thoughts she was having to 'listen' to. Brezhnev had stopped everyone from making purchases of food and other things in shops, and she had decided to rebel, hence her 'delinquent act'. At times she 'became' her sister, experiencing her emotions and sensations (appersonation). One day while 'babysitting' for this sister, who had gone to the theatre, she felt her sister had transformed herself into her, Fiona (transitivism), so that she could take her place on a television show with Prince Charles.

Once again there was a gradual improvement, with the disappearance of the delusional ideas. The hallucinatory experiences receded in intensity but did not actually disappear. Fiona remained at home, being able to undertake household tasks and mix with her family, but unable to work.

(ii) In paranoid psychoses
No case available for presentation.

(b) Persecutory delusions preceded by erotomania
(i) In schizophrenic psychoses
Persecutory delusions which follow erotomania in cases of schizophrenia may continue unaltered for years, and this was so in the case of May. The delusional ideas may be sufficiently encapsulated from the remainder of healthy mental life as to allow the patient a limited degree of environmental adjustment.

In other cases the delusional content changes, and the original male persecutor gives way to another male persecutor. For example, Eve, an unmarried woman of 26, developed an erotomania while under treatment for depressive symptoms. Shortly after beginning the psychotherapy she declared her love for the psychiatrist, who regarded this phenomenon as transference love (Freud, 1915a). Her condition improved, but it was impossible to get her to examine her love or to appreciate that her idealization of the psychiatrist was inappropriate. Eve was disturbed if she thought that he was less than attentive, and after a session during which she reproached him for not showing the love which she was convinced he had for her she made a suicidal attempt. She was then admitted to hospital, where the psychotherapy continued. However, Eve continued to insist that the psychiatrist was in love with her but for some reason, unknown to her, had to remain silent.

The psychiatrist left to work in another hospital. Some weeks later Eve told a nurse that she had received a letter implying that she, Eve, had had a sexual affair with the psychiatrist, and this evoked great anger. Soon she claimed that he had seduced her, made her pregnant and then caused her to have an abortion. Men kept looking at her, some making sexual advances to her; she was aware of sexual feelings being imposed on her. The psychiatrist had turned her into a prostitute, and she accused him of indulging in an unnatural sexual practice (coitus per anum) and telling everyone that she was a homosexual.

If Eve suspected that the listener to her story was unsympathetic, she became angry and sullen, and for many months she remained in a withdrawn state, refusing to talk to anyone. A pronounced negativism appeared. After about a year, however, the medical director of the hospital came to replace the psychiatrist as persecutor. Now she said she was the daughter of George VI, and that the man and woman who brought her up were not her real parents. She refused to communicate with them. In her dealings with doctors, nurses and other patients Eve was arrogant and overbearing, and, if addressed by her real name, fell into a rage in which she accused the medical staff of preventing her real identity from being disclosed. These delusional ideas receded with medications but she remained withdrawn and hypochondriacal over the next number of years.

The theme of jealousy is confined to cases where erotomania is followed by persecution by a member of the same sex. In some cases the persecution is continued by the former 'lover' in collaboration with a woman known to the patient before she fell ill. In the case of Christine described earlier, for instance, the persecution was carried out by a female cousin who looked after the patient when she first fell ill, while the original beloved was made an accomplice.

At the onset an erotomania gives no indication as to the course of the illness. The delusional ideas which replace the erotomania, wholly or in part, may recede, with the patient being able to lead a normal life. Erotomania and its sequelae (delusions, etc.) can recur after a remission which had lasted for some years, and patients who have such remissions are to be contrasted with those (see the cases of May, Christine and Eve) where the persecutory complex, which follows the erotomania, becomes a permanent feature of the patient's mental life (moderate to severe end state, Bleuler, M., 1978).

(ii) In paranoid psychoses
So called 'pure' erotomania (Enoch and Trethowen, 1979) has always been categorized within the group of paranoid psychoses. The adjective 'pure' has been used to describe the fact that in these cases the erotomania is not followed by persecution by a known man or woman. Generally cases of 'pure' erotomania undergo a remission which may be permanent or recur.

(c) Persecutory delusions alone
(i) In schizophrenic psychoses
The case of a female patient who at the onset of the illness believed herself to be persecuted by a man is illustrated by Kath. The content in cases of this type is usually of a sexual nature and here there is no belief in being loved (i.e. no erotomania), but rather a sense of oppression by the 'lies' told about the person by the persecutor or by the alien sexual feelings and thoughts which he causes her to experience. As in the case of Kath, there is usually at least one remission after the first attack. In her case, in fact, a second attack followed within the year, but with a different presentation. Withdrawal, negativism and unpredictable behaviour were its predominant features, while self-neglect, irritability, negativism and catatonic signs became the outstanding features in the chronic condition (a severe end state).

(ii) In paranoid psychoses
The delusion of being persecuted by a known member of the opposite sex without preceding wish delusions or erotomania is a common presentation in paranoid psychoses (see the preceding chapter). The course of the illness may be towards recovery, recurrence or chronicity.

Persecution by unknown persons or agencies

(a) Persecutory delusions preceded or accompanied by wish delusions
(i) In schizophrenic psychoses
Wilson, an unmarried man, fell ill at the age of 20. (His case is described in the Appendix.) Wilson's illness followed a cyclical course, of a kind not uncommon in this type of schizophrenia where there are wish delusions without a serious 'deterioration' of the personality. Wilson went back to work but in the following years abandoned jobs, until a time came when he could not get work; there were occasional periods of delusional thinking.

(ii) In paranoid psychoses
The case of Derek is typical of this form of paranoid psychotic illness. The outcome in his case was suicide, because the dread of the persecutors reached such intensity that he killed himself; fortunately the anxiety is not always so intense and there is progress to remission. For example, Deirdre, a 41-year-old unmarried woman, believed that she had been recruited to assist in defeating the IRA, and that she was in telepathic communication with the Secret Service. When admitted to hospital she said that she was magnetized, and that if she came into contact with metals electrical impulses passed through her body. Deirdre became very frightened when she formed the idea that the IRA were about to blow up her house and kill her. Her instructions from the Secret Service, she explained, had not come by way of a voice in her head, but through a mechanism by which her thoughts appeared to be mixed up with those of another person (transitivism).

This attack was provoked by a transient and disappointing

love affair with a man. However, the delusional attack subsided, and six years later Deirdre had not had a relapse into illness: she had continued with her work and led a reasonably normal life.

(b) Persecutory delusions alone
(i) In schizophrenic psychoses
In schizophrenic psychoses which begin with persecutory delusions alone, the course is often one to a moderately severe or severe end state. The case of Ann is illustrative here, while the case of Harry is typical of those which follow a cyclical course without serious 'deterioration' of the personality. The trend towards remission without further attacks is more common in cases where there are also wish delusions, for instance, Peter's case.

(ii) In paranoid psychoses
The outcome in paranoid psychoses, where there are only persecutory delusions, is often to chronicity, and here the case of Joan is illustrative. Joan's delusions remained unaltered, so that nine years after the onset she continued to blame persecutors for her distressing bodily experiences.

A cyclical course is also not uncommon. For example, Roberta, a 50-year-old married woman, was admitted to hospital because she complained of being victimized by unknown persons whom she believed to be friends of people she had unwittingly offended. After a month or so these ideas disappeared, but Roberta was readmitted four months later with identical symptoms. Her case is of interest because the therapist, during psychotherapeutic treatment, became the centre of a delusional complex. Roberta complained that he had her under a hypnotic spell, and was the agent of her persecutors, being responsible for her lack of skin sensation, for her lack of emotions, for putting obscene thoughts in her head, and for arranging for her to be sexually assaulted while asleep. Gradually these ideas disappeared as the underlying causes for the illness became manifest. This was an act of infidelity – coitus with a friend of her son.

In the case of Roberta a depressive element characterized by self-reproaches was to be noted, and depressive manifestations occur frequently in paranoid psychoses. Cases are occasionally encountered where the persecutory attack follows one or more depressive attacks: for example, Don, a married man of 46, complained of depression of mood, and was self-reproachful. Although he recovered with electroshock therapy, he had to be readmitted to hospital three months later with similar symptoms. On a third admission the depressive manifestations seemed less pronounced, and now he appeared to act in a suspicious manner. Someone – he did not know who it was – was interfering with his affairs, opening his letters, etc. Someone had stolen his birth certificate; the Freemasons were conspiring to ruin him.

Don's persecutory delusions subsided after eight months and he was discharged from hospital. Once again, however, he had to be readmitted because the radio was broadcasting 'lies' about him. Someone was putting thoughts into his head and taking them out again, and he heard voices calling him a cheat and a liar. Gradually the persecutory phenomena receded and Don was discharged; more than two years later he was still free of delusions. Periodically he had felt low-spirited but not sufficiently to stop him working.

· Changes in delusional content during the course of the illness

(a) In schizophrenia
Changes in delusional content occur almost universally in those cases of schizophrenia which terminate in moderate to severe end states (Bleuler, M., 1978), and here the cases of Edith, Sheila, Tom, Kath, Henry, Ann, Christine and Fiona are illustrative. It is also interesting to note that the content of Schreber's delusions (Freud, 1911) altered dramatically as his illness continued. At the onset Schreber was persecuted by Fleschig, his doctor; later by God, but within the context of a grandiose delusional complex. Changes of this kind are commonplace in schizophrenic patients where persecutory delusions play a prominent part at the onset of the illness: the cases of Emma,

Christine and Eve are illustrative in this respect. Where the psychosis follows a cyclical course (schizophrenic psychoses), the content in later attacks may be identical to that in the first (see the case of William), or there may be slight variations on the original theme (see the case of Wilson).

(b) In paranoid psychoses
In paranoid psychoses the content of delusions may remain constant in attacks after a remission, or, as in the case of Charles (Chapter 2), there may be a change. Here the unknown persecutors in the first two attacks were replaced by a known persecutor (his brother). In female patients, on the other hand, it is not uncommon to find that the persecutor in the first attack is a woman, in subsequent attacks a man – this was so in the case of Sheila (Chapter 2).

CHAPTER 4

Pre-psychotic identifications and their vicissitudes in the schizophrenias

D
URING psychoanalytic work with cases of anxiety hysteria, and in some character disorders, it is possible to observe how symptoms and disadvantageous (reactive) personality traits arise from the transformation of the aims and objects of wishes through secondary identification. These reversals of aim and replacements of elements of the self by aspects of the object are gradually brought into the patient's consciousness through the medium of the transference. This process, in turn, reveals the nature of the danger situations and conflicts of childhood which led to the pathological transformation of instinctual wishes by way of identification. Identifications which can be discerned in the pre-psychotic phase (Katan, 1954) of the schizophrenias appear to have similar origins, but with the onset of the psychotic attack they become subject to the effects of psychical dissolution.

Many psychoanalysts, following Tausk (1919) and Nunberg (1921), have shown that the transitivism, appersonation (Bleuler, 1924), and passivity experiences which occur in the schizophrenias can be attributed to a form of identification, variously described as psychotic (Jacobson, 1954), narcissistic (Nunberg, 1921) and primitive (Frosch, 1983). The most obvious instances of this form of identification are to be found in cases where an acute psychotic attack has followed the loss of a real love object (Tausk, 1919; Freeman, 1981a), but this primitive or psychotic identification is also a feature of the hebephrenic-catatonic type of chronic schizophrenia (Freeman, Cameron and McGhie, 1958).

At the onset of an acute psychotic attack the patient is preoccupied with his delusional and hallucinatory experiences. His attention does not spontaneously turn to the period prior to the onset of the symptoms, as it does in anxiety hysteria. However, Katan (1974, 1975, 1979) has demonstrated that the phenomena of the acute attack can provide important data about the patient's object relationships in the period immediately preceding the break with reality (the pre-psychotic phase). Additional information is also available from the neurotic-like symptoms which so frequently occur prior to the psychotic attack. In these studies of the pre-psychotic phase attention must be given to the variety of clinical phenomena and courses of illness which characterize the schizophrenias. Thus in this respect the phenomena described in Chapter 2 are of importance, particularly the affects of envy and jealousy, whether the persecutor is personally known or not; whether, if known, of the same or opposite sex; and, lastly, if the persecutory manifestations are preceded or accompanied by grandiose (wish) delusions.

The two patients now to be described were seen regularly in psychotherapeutic sessions, but the clinical material is limited to that relevant for the subject of this presentation. In the first case, that of William (Chapter 2), grandiose (wish) delusions were followed by persecutory manifestations, and here the persecutor was a real person – William's brother. The illness followed a cyclical course, with relapses and remissions, while the delusional content in relapses was the same as that in the first acute attack. In periods of remission William's personality was little different from that prior to the first attack. The initial presentation in the second case (see the case of Emma, Chapter 2) was of persecutory delusions and a transient erotomania. There were two persecutors, neither being known to the patient. As the illness proceeded the first (male) persecutor faded into the background, to be replaced by the second (female). Another male persecutor later made an appearance (see page 54), and there was a gradual alteration in the personality in the direction of withdrawal, loss of volition and periodic acute attacks.

William was admitted to hospital because his speech and behaviour were disturbed: he had threatened to kill his brother, who was some years older than himself. William's parents reported that he had been unusually cheerful during the previous weeks, claiming that several girls were competing to marry him. He also announced that he had been specially selected to participate in an important research project. But shortly after arriving in hospital he attacked a male nurse because he thought the nurse was suggesting they had a homosexual relationship. William also said that his brother was causing him to have homosexual thoughts; his brother was following him everywhere and had taken to dressing exactly as he, William, did, copying his gestures and manner. William then claimed that his brother was intent on seducing his sister and, out of envy, as mentioned before, wished to get him out of the way so that he could inherit the family property when their father died.

The beginning of the process of illness – the pre-psychotic phase – can be traced to William's brother's announcement that he was to be married. Psychotherapeutic work with this young man revealed that he had always been shy and retiring by nature: although attracted to girls he lacked the self-confidence to strike up a relationship with them. He compulsively masturbated but was left with a sense of shame and guilt, and during the pre-psychotic phase his masturbatory conflict intensified. At the time of the psychotic attack he regarded masturbation as a crime which led to homosexuality, but as far as he was concerned he was entirely heterosexual.

The data which emerged during the treatment confirmed the hypothesis, formed on the basis of the delusional content (see Chapter 2), that in the pre-psychotic phase William identified with his brother: he wished to be him and possess all that he possessed. The active aim of the pre-psychotic wish phantasy was expressed, by projection, in the delusional idea that it was his brother who wanted to kill him and commit incest with their sister. The pre-psychotic dread of giving way to masturbation resulted from the fear that, in experiencing genital excitement, the phantasy of killing his brother and committing incest with his sister would reach consciousness. In the acute attack the dissolution of mental life gave these pre-psychotic wishes a psychical reality.

The fear of retribution which began in the pre-psychotic phase became conscious in the psychotic attack in the form of the dread that the brother wanted to rob him of his masculinity (castration), and turn him into a woman (homosexuality). In this case the terror of homosexuality did not arise from a passive feminine wish phantasy, as can be demonstrated in other schizophrenic patients; here, rather, it was the dread of castration at the hands of the person (the brother) he wished to be. It was a matter of being rather than having the love object (Freud, 1921).

In the case of Emma (see Chapter 2) the illness declared itself when Emma complained that she was being victimized by a man who had been in her class at university the previous year. (She had only known him by sight.) He was slandering her through wireless and television. Nevertheless he loved her, and if he did not come to visit it was because his mother was jealous. His mother (whom she did not know) hated her.

After some weeks Emma came to the conclusion that the man was persecuting her because she had ignored him at university. She recalled seeing his desire for her on his face, and whatever was happening now to him was also happening to her. She believed that he had made himself mentally ill (transitivism) through behaving as he had done (i.e. masturbating). She was now suffering mentally too. By this she meant that she was tense, restless and low-spirited. She said that she and the young man were physically alike – 'I look like him, tall and fair-haired. He has a round face [like herself] and gives you a long look. I find myself doing that' (appersonation).

In the year preceding the acute attack Emma had a boyfriend, her first, but after some months she stopped the relationship: she told her mother that he wanted to have intercourse and she could not agree. During psychotherapeutic sessions Emma said that she did not like the idea of intercourse – it seemed bestial to her, and this revelation fitted well with what she later expressed. Throughout childhood Emma had wanted to be a boy: she played boys' games and later spent much of her free time in athletic pursuits. She also reported, confirming her mother's memory, that she hated her young and only brother. She recalled saying 'I don't want him.' Later, however, her attitude changed, and she became protective towards him. Thus through identification with her mother, and putting herself in her brother's place, she unconsciously satisfied the double wish of having her mother to herself and of being a boy. She also remembered playing doctor games with her brother, in which she took the active (doctor) role. Vague recollections of seeing her father's penis were probably elements of a prolonged phallic phase.

As Emma did not know her persecutor(s) – the fellow student and his mother – they must be regarded as substitutes and taken to represent her real boyfriend and his mother (whom she did know) in the present, and her brother and mother in the past. For throughout the lengthy period of psychotherapeutic contact Emma never talked about her real boyfriend and her experiences with him. Even when questioned, her thoughts wandered to one or other of her delusional ideas. Her psychical experiences of the male persecutor suggest that the morbid process, which culminated in the psychotic attack, began with the sexual encounters with her first boyfriend. In this pre-psychotic phase clitoral excitability led to revival of her childhood phallic sexuality, with its wishes for a penis and the mother as love object. Emma was thus unconsciously envious of her boyfriend's masculinity, and jealous of his relationship with his mother. She wanted to turn his mother against him by telling her about the love-making (reference the delusional idea of being slandered). If she could not have her (the mother), neither would he.

In the pre-psychotic phase Emma fulfilled her unconscious wish to be a man through identification with the real boyfriend. Elements of this identification were simultaneously projected on to the boyfriend. He wanted her sexually. In this way, then, the danger provoked by her masturbatory (homosexual) wish phantasy was temporarily relieved. The pre-psychotic identification therefore acted as a defence as well as a means of wish-fulfilment.

With the dissolution of the ego (the psychotic attack) and the emergence of the primary process, the real boyfriend and his mother were replaced by the delusional boyfriend and his mother. The memories and the wishes of the real sexual encounters they provoked were now deprived access to consciousness. The delusional content (via projection) suggests that Emma, when with her real boyfriend, played or wished to play the active part in love-making. In doing so she excited him to erection and emission, thus completing her identification with him and simultaneously depriving him of his potency.

Further delusional contents indicate that this wish evoked anxiety of such intensity as to precipitate the psychotic attack. Emma claimed that a man who owned a trucking business next door to her father's office, where she did a little work, had punished his young male employees in a particularly horrible manner. He stripped them of their clothes, bundled them into an open truck and drove them around the town for everyone to see; she feared he was going to do this to her. She thought she had always known about this kind of punishment for misdeeds – parents did this to boys who were disobedient. This was to be her punishment. As a man she must suffer the punishment that is inflicted on men because of their misdeeds.

Dissolution of the personality led to a psychotic identification, with its merging of the physical and mental aspects of the self and the delusional substitute. The sexual (masturbatory) excitement generated by her masculinity was now embodied in the persecutor and the fiction of her heterosexuality could be maintained. As the illness proceeded the substitute mother became the principal persecutor according to the formula, 'I do not love her, I hate her, she hates me.'

These two patients differed markedly in the way they behaved and related during the psychotherapeutic sessions. Emma's were held twice a week and, during a period of hospitalization, five times a week. Now she was entirely preoccupied with her delusional and hallucinatory experiences – her impressions of daily life and recollections of the past were always expressed in the context of the delusional ideas. Any suggestion that thoughts or memories reflected a preconscious thought about the author never met with a response. Emma was well disposed to him and looked to him to help resist the pressure of the persecutors; throughout the treatment period there was no evidence of a failure of self-object discrimination with respect to the author. (This was confined to the male persecutor.) The distress evoked by the mysterious happenings and her attempts to explain them must have reflected some earlier lack of understanding, but presenting this process as a repetitive manifestation failed to evoke a response. In contrast to William, Emma was never anxious in the treatment sessions: this fact again detracted from the likelihood that the writer was unconsciously conceived of as a persecuting figure. Thus, 'interpretations' based on such an idea again met with no reaction.

William was seen twice a week, and five times a week during periods in hospital; he responded actively to the author from the start. In the grandiose phases of the illness he was elated and self-confident, and at the onset said that the author was a homosexual. William objected to him sitting with his legs crossed because a girl he knew, who excited him to masturbation, had sat that way. Soon, however, he became anxious: the author was trying to turn him into a homosexual by making him feel like a woman. As with his brother he first acquired the author's masculinity and turned him into a woman. This psychotic identification with the author, however, was swept away by the fear of the consequences of this violent, acquisitive act – being castrated and turned into a woman.

It is usually impossible to witness, at first hand, the transition from the pre-psychotic phase to the psychosis, because of the brevity of the former. However, there are patients whose pre-psychotic symptoms lead them to seek psychiatric treatment, so the acute attack makes its appearance while they are under observation. In the following instance (see the case of Christine,

PP-E

Chapter 3), the pre-psychotic phase lasted for more than a year, and the pre-psychotic symptom followed from object choice to identification. As this schizophrenic illness progressed there was a change in the content of the delusions.

Christine became depressed after her fiancé ended their engagement. She gradually recovered, only to fall ill some months later, now blaming herself for the breakdown of the relationship. Her self-criticisms were such as to leave no doubt that they expressed her anger against the fiancé. A concomitant change in manner added further weight to the conclusion that she had identified with the lost love object. Then after some months the depressive manifestations gave way to the delusion that her former fiancé was trying to contact her. He had made a mistake, not appreciating how much he loved her. Someone was preventing her from meeting her fiancé. Christine became progressively withdrawn and had to be admitted to hospital. Now she heard her fiancé's voice, and accused a female cousin of preventing her from seeing him because she, the cousin, was jealous.

As described in Chapter 3, Christine developed an attachment to a male doctor, who took the place of the former fiancé when he left the hospital. She now claimed that her female cousin, out of jealousy, had enlisted the support of her former fiancé to stop her beloved doctor from seeing her. In spite of all forms of treatment, this delusion continued unremitting over very many years.

During the pre-psychotic phase Christine had identified with her lover. This led to a revival of phallic homosexual wishes based on a strong libidinal fixation to her young sister, to whom she had been devoted. After her disappointment in love she wished to turn once again to her sister, but the latter was now married. A danger situation had been created by her homosexual wishes and by her jealousy of her brother-in-law. Thus soon after the onset of the psychosis a female persecutor appeared on the scene, who was 'jealous' of Christine. During the psychosis belief in her heterosexuality could continue through the wish phantasy of her lover's attempts to find her once more; as time passed a new phantasy lover was discovered, and the homosexual cathexis was transferred to a substitute – the female cousin. The jealousy, no longer repressed as it had been in the pre-psychotic phase, was projected. In order to maintain the 'repression' of the homosexuality love turned to hate – 'I do not love her, I hate her, she hates me out of jealousy.'

In the cases described there was no difference between the origins and purposes of the pre-psychotic identifications, although the courses of illness varied. In the young man, where the course was one of remissions and relapses without damage to the personality, the object relationship, represented in the pre-psychotic identification, was observed in the transitivism and appersonation of the acute attack (psychotic identification). In the women patients, the psychotic identification was with a substitute for the real object relationship of the pre-psychotic phase.

The psychotic identification in these cases served the same purposes (wish-fulfilment, defence, etc.) as did the identifica-tions of the pre-psychotic phase. However, as these observations have been derived from a small number of schizophrenic patients, it would be wrong to conclude that all remitting cases of schizophrenia are characterized, at the onset of the illness, by a psychotic identification with a real love object; and that all cases which terminate in 'end states' are characterized by psychotic identifications with substitute objects.

On the other hand, the observations described do prompt the following hypothesis based on Freud's (1924) theory of schizophrenia. When the psychotic identification is with a real person of affective significance to the patient, the object is retained despite the dissolution of psychical structure and the resultant condensation of self and object representations caused by the intrusion of the primary process. When the psychotic identification occurs with a substitute (phantasy) object, the dissolution has set free the means of substitution, namely displacement (primary process, Freud, 1900). There is a displacement from real self and object images, as represented in the pre-psychotic identifications, to substitutes as occurred in the two female patients. This displacement took place immediately in the case of Emma and gradually in the case of Christine.

This hypothesis is supported by what was observed during the treatment sessions. In the case of William the author was implicated in a psychotic identification. The cathexis of real objects (writer, brother) was maintained in the face of a dissolution which led to the primitive form of object relationship (the psychotic identification). But in the case of Emma, the author was never a part of the psychotic identification: he was without affective significance because the cathexis of real objects had already been displaced to substitutes.

As the morbid process advances in such cases primitive, magical phantasies of the self, undifferentiated from one another (Bychowski, 1952; Jacobson, 1967; Freeman, 1969), replace real self and object representations in that part of the mind affected by the psychosis. These psychotic identifications reflect the extent to which real objects have been given up (decathexis) and a new reality constructed (Freud, 1924; Frosch, 1983). According to this hypothesis the course which a schizophrenic psychosis will follow is less dependent on the depth of psychical dissolution at the onset than it is on the extent to which object ties (object cathexis) can resist the influence of displacement (primary process).

CHAPTER 5

The contents of delusions and hysterical phantasies

T HE SUBJECT of the content of delusions and hysterical phantasies attracted the attention of the first generation of psychoanalysts. Apart from the references which Freud made to this topic, a number of important contributions are to be found in the early psychoanalytic literature (Abraham, 1907a, 1907b; Jung, 1907). Since those days many new analytic concepts have been introduced, and these have had a particular influence on psychoanalytic theorizing about the psychoses. This chapter consists of a study of the similarities and differences which exist between delusional contents and hysterical phantasies in the light of these recent theoretical ideas.

The contents of delusions

In female patients, as Bleuler (1911) originally pointed out, erotic ideas frequently comprise the content of persecutory delusions. In one group of patients there are coital, or rape and pregnancy delusions. The stimulus for these phenomena can be found in a patient's infatuation with a man she knows personally, whom she only knows by sight or has read about, heard or seen on radio or television. In the case of Eve (see Chapter 3), these delusions arose in the context of a psychotherapeutic relationship. Eve accused the psychiatrist of having seduced her without her knowledge and making her pregnant. In a mysterious way he had caused her to have an abortion. Then at a later stage, as already described, the medical director of the hospital, a man of her father's age, took the place of the first persecutor.

Delusions of being raped and impregnated are, as in the case described, frequently preceded by erotomania. In one category of cases, the beloved is transformed into a persecutor (the case of Eve). In another category of cases characterized by a 'love triangle' the delusions consist of phantasies which depict a sexual encounter (coitus) between the patient and her beloved: the other woman initiates a secret surveillance to seek revenge on the patient. In still other cases where there is a love triangle the patient is forced to endure the love-making of her male and female persecutors. An instance of the former is provided by the case of Nan, the 30-year-old unmarried woman (see Chapter 2) whose acute attack occurred during group psychotherapy. An example of the latter is the case of Christine (see Chapter 3), an unmarried woman of 23 who became seriously depressed after her fiancé broke off the engagement to marry.

The barely hidden incestuous wish phantasies found in the case of Eve are often openly expressed in those patients whose illness begins in early or middle adolescence. One common delusion is of being sexually abused by the father; sometimes there is the delusion of having had a child by the father. For example, Ann (see Chapter 2) claimed that her youngest brother was her child. She said, '. . . my father is a prince, I have a son by him, he was born when I was 14 [her age when she fell ill and when her mother was pregnant] . . . my son is doing his job at the university [her brother, now aged 19, was at university]. It was explained to me, what else could he be but my son.'

In all the sexual delusions the patient rages against the persecutor(s), male, female or both, because of their power to induce clitoral excitement and to tempt her to masturbate. This is also the case with the prostitution phantasies which play a prominent role in these delusions. The patient angrily claims that she is powerless to stop numerous men from having intercourse with her, because of the persecutor's malevolent actions. This may take the form of an hypnotic influence; in other cases the delusion is limited to the idea that she hears others call her a prostitute.

Sometimes, too, a fear of being murdered is a prominent feature of the content of delusions, and the fear is frequently connected with phantasy or real sexual experiences. In the case of Deirdre (Chapter 3), the delusion of being about to be murdered followed a sexual experience. Deirdre met a man, was fascinated by him, and they were sexually intimate. At the time she experienced the excitement as magnetic in quality, although she was unable to explain what she meant. Following this she felt herself to be united with him, in the sense of experiencing his thoughts and feelings, and almost participating in his actions, despite the fact that they were hundreds of miles apart. At times she felt as if she were two people, she and the man. Deirdre said, at the time of her hospital admission, that she had been subjected to a magnetic process which enabled her to anticipate and detect the activities of terrorists. They were going to kill her before she could contact the authorities.

Saviour delusions are sometimes to be observed in female patients. The woman may believe herself to be Christ, or that she has been entrusted with a mission – to save humanity or direct individuals towards a moral life. This was so with Mary (Chapter 2), who believed that she had to rescue a male cousin, whom she had not seen for some years, from a life of sexual depravity. Not uncommonly the wish delusion is replaced by persecution – anxiety takes the place of elation. A young woman of 19 ecstatically declared that Christ was to be reborn, and that her task was to announce this to the world. A short time later, however, she feared she was to be murdered.

Finally, reference must be made to the family romance phantasies (Freud, 1909) which occur so commonly as part of the content of schizophrenic delusions. These have both wish and persecutory elements respectively: there is the denial of the real parents and the claim of an exalted parentage; the patient also complains that an enemy prevents her 'true' identity from being revealed: it is for this reason that she is imprisoned in the hospital. With female patients the enemy is the mother or sister, or an obvious substitute for them.

In male patients phantasies of ambitions fulfilled comprise much of the content of delusions, yet as Bleuler (1911) pointed out, erotic ideas also occur. Indeed, these two elements are frequently in combination. Tom, for example (Chapter 2), believed that reunion with his imaginary beloved was only prevented by the failure of the authorities to recognize their monetary obligations to him for reconstructing the hospital after its (imagined) destruction. When a patient believes that he has great achievements to his credit he may simultaneously claim that he is being cheated of the rewards of his labours by his father or brother. Henry (Chapter 2) believed that he had discovered a means of providing a new source of energy which made oil and coal superfluous, but through envy his father had stolen the plans of his invention. His father, he said, had committed a murder, but the police could not find the body and so could not proceed against him. James (Chapter 2) believed that his father had tried to kill him because he was envious of his youthful strength and stamina. On the other hand, the evil and wicked father is very often represented by a substitute. Peter, for instance (Chapter 2), claimed that he had designed pieces of scientific equipment with which he could demolish a theory advanced by a distinguished research worker. He had under-taken this task because the man was an evil influence on mankind in general, and, with his accomplices, was trying to destroy Peter's plans by spreading a rumour that he was a homosexual.

Actual or hoped-for material possessions, rather than phantasy ambitions fulfilled, are sometimes, in the patient's opinion, the cause of a brother's envy and hatred. Illustrative is the case of Charles described in Chapter 2. As mentioned then, Charles was accusing his wife of poisoning him. (He and his wife were childless.) He said that his older brother had forced his wife to poison him by threatening to expose the fact that she had had a child by another man prior to her marriage. In another case the patient claimed that his brother was vilifying him as a homosexual and degenerate, so that their father would disown him and cut him out of the father's will. In addition to these delusional phantasies of family relationships there are also those, as in the case of female patients, where the real parents are denied and others proclaimed as parents who are more in accord with the patient's wishes.

There are cases where jealousy as well as envy can be identified by the patient as the cause of his persecution, and here the erotic element is discernible; James, in Chapter 2, is illustrative. Some weeks prior to the attack he began to believe that a woman colleague had fallen in love with him. A few days before he had been at lunch when the two men he later believed wished to kill him entered the restaurant. He thought they might be the woman's father or brother, and began to wonder if the father or brother or both were jealous because the daughter/sister had fallen in love with him. They now wanted to get rid of him.

Rape phantasies are also to be found in male patients, and when they occur they are usually of an active character. The patient either believes that he is being calumnated as a rapist, or that he has raped women unknowingly while under the malign influence of persecutors. In these instances the patient also claims that the rape scene has been recorded by electronic devices, data which will be used to blackmail him or given to the police so that he can be prosecuted. These ideas cause anxiety and agitation. Then in some instances the patient complains of having been raped per anum. In one case this phantasy was accompanied by the idea that people in the street were saying that the man was a homosexual. Wilson (Chapter 3) claimed that God had penetrated him anally while he was in the bath.

In those cases where the delusional content consists of a conflict with the father or a father substitute, as in two of the male patients described above, there is also a delusion about homosexuality. The latter may consist in the idea of being turned into a woman: for example, one man believed that the archbishop of his church was not the person he appeared to be. An evil man had assumed his appearance and identity, and killed the real archbishop. This evil man knew that the patient had discovered his secret, and in order to discredit him was trying to turn him into a woman; the patient could feel it happening to him

– at times his body was so affected that he walked with a woman's gait. But at the same time, he was not disturbed by the contradictory belief, provoked by a hallucinated voice, that God had ordained that he, as a woman, was to repopulate the world with good people.

Bleuler (1911), Jung (1907) and Abraham (1907b) discerned that wish phantasies are an intrinsic element of delusions. Although the experience of persecution is often the initial manifestation of a schizophrenic illness, it is essentially a reaction to a wish phantasy. Now according to Bleuler (1911) the development of persecutory ideas occurs whenever an obstacle blocks the fulfilment of a wish. The persecutory experience becomes manifest when the obstacle opposing wish-fulfilment or the delusion of a fulfilled wish is heightened. In Bleuler's (1911) words '. . . aspirations must conceal themselves behind delusions of persecution . . . the wish is the primary element.' According to Bleuler (1911) negative feeling tones evoked by wish-fulfilment are the source of these intrapsychic obstacles. It has also long been recognized that wish phantasies, identical to those which lead to the experience of persecution in the schizophrenias, are to be found during the psychoanalytic treatment of hysterical neuroses (anxiety and conversion hysteria) (Freud, 1908).

Hysterical phantasies

Those like Bleuler, Jung and Abraham, who pioneered the psychoanalytic study of the schizophrenias, described the similarities which exist between hysterical phantasies and delusional content. In this they profited from Freud's discovery of a causal connection between hysterical symptoms and phantasies. Of particular importance was Freud's discovery (1908) that in some hysterical neuroses homosexual phantasies played a significant role in the creation of the symptoms. During psychoanalytic treatment these phantasies, both heterosexual and homosexual, are the cause of resistances, amongst which acting out in the transference is prominent.

As the resistances are overcome it is the erotic, heterosexual phantasies which first come to light. For example, a male patient of 33 suffering from an anxiety hysteria had the following phantasy on his way to the analytic session. He is driving his car, which collides with another in which a man is driving, accompanied by a woman. The couple are trapped in the car. The patient ignores the man and rescues the woman, comforts her and then makes love to her. Then, however, he has to go to court to face a charge of dangerous driving. The prosecutor tries to trap him with his questions, but the patient gets the better of him and is exonerated; he has a sense of triumph. In masturbatory phantasy he meets a woman, and obtains a hold over her through discovering an indiscretion. He blackmails her into having coitus.

A counterpart to these phantasies were frightening thoughts connected with the author. The patient feared that there were electronic devices in the room, and that he would incriminate himself. The author would have him trapped and blackmail him, and would also stick a knife into his back as he walked into the consulting room. In the course of relating the heterosexual phantasies the patient thought of his wife and himself having coitus; but then he thought of his wife having intercourse with the author. An image of the latter's penis came to mind, and then the patient had the phantasy of a woman becoming excited as she expressed sexual thoughts, as he was now doing in the session.

This man was frightened by his passive feminine wishes. Unconsciously he was the trapped, blackmailed woman who would have to succumb to the analyst and submit to a homosexual attack. In this case the active (heterosexual) and passive (homosexual) phantasies gave expression to identification with both parents in the act of intercourse. In another case, the emergence of homosexual wish phantasies from behind a screen of erotic heterosexuality was also to be observed in a female patient of hysterical personality type. After the resolution of a resistance caused by identification with the aggressor (Freud, A., 1936), she was able to reveal a complex of erotic phantasies, dormant amongst which were phantasies of prostitution and of being raped. In her sexual life she was vaginally anaesthetic, but she could obtain some sexual (clitoric) excitement by picturing her lover making love to another woman; the excitement was heightened if she could get her lover to tell her of his actual experiences when making love with someone else. Resistance led to her acting out the erotic phantasies in real life.

Then a dream brought final confirmation of the phallic-homosexual orientation of her libido, evidence of which had been accumulating over a long period of time. In the first place, during the dream day, she experienced intense sexual frustration. Then in the dream the son of a woman friend appeared to be sexually excited, telling her that he pushes his erect penis into soft objects when he has no other outlet. She has the thought, 'I have nothing which I can use to push into things.' In the prostitution and rape phantasies she was (unconsciously) the man: the client in the former, the rapist in the latter. Transference phantasies of sexually assaulting the author, uncovered after the resolution of much resistance, gave expression to her phallic masculinity, as well as to an identification with her father in coitus with her mother, with whom she was also identified.

Introversion and regression

In common with other cases of hysteria, the patients described above turned to phantasy (introversion, Freud, 1916) in the face of what was for them an unsatisfying reality. In the case of the woman it was not so much a matter of being deprived of opportunities for satisfaction, but rather that she was unable to avail herself of those opportunities open to her. In the case of the man this factor also played a part but, additionally, he had to contend with an actual (contemporary) frustration.

Through the medium of the transference, as has already been intimated, and through the recovery of memories, it was possible to construct the fixations to which the libido had regressed, and in so doing creating the childhood prototypes of the phantasy contents which have been described. Both patients were fixated to incestuous objects of their own sex, and this had precluded the full development of their heterosexuality. The woman patient's fixation to the mother as an Oedipal object was established during the pre-Oedipal period when oral- and anal-sadistic preoccupations, largely provoked by environmental interferences (Nagera, 1966), created predominantly external conflicts and anxiety. At entry into the phallic phase these pregenital, sadistic influences heightened penis envy and led to castration wishes. A phallic masculinity was established with the mother as love object, but this was screened by an apparent movement towards the father. In fact this movement was based on narcissism (the wish to be a man), rather than on true object choice.

As to the male patient, a combination of maternal overstimulation and overprotection led to developmental conflicts (Freud, A., 1965), particularly in the sphere of anal sadism. This led to the heightening of passive sexual aims, on the one side, and reaction formations, on the other. There evolved throughout this period an identification with the mother, which led to the assimilation of certain of her neurotic symptoms. Yet despite these occurrences, a progression to the Oedipus phase, to active sexual aims and to a heterosexual object took place. These developmental achievements were only precariously held, however, as further events were to show. The potential for regression was always present, with object choice early reverting to identification, activity being replaced by passivity, and masturbatory excitement by anal 'excitation' – the latter demonstrated in (periodic) childhood faecal incontinence.

In psychoses one sees a more obvious turning from reality to phantasy – introversion – the introversion sometimes being a reaction to a reality that is, in fact, unsatisfying. Rachael (see Chapter 2), for example, became alternately withdrawn in manner and impulsive in her behaviour. On the one hand, she neglected her domestic duties and, on the other, unpredictably attacked her husband with a knife. Some four years previously she had been hospitalized because of similar behaviour. On that occasion she complained that a man with whom she had kept company years earlier, and had hoped to marry, stood outside her house every night. The words Rachael heard him say indicated to her that he must be in a state of sexual excitement: it was his intention to excite her and she bitterly resented this.

When admitted to hospital for the second time Rachael acted erotically, misidentifying the author and a male nurse as the man in question. She repeated her delusional accusations that the author, in the shape of her former lover, was causing her to experience genital excitement, and during these disturbed states gave expression to the following thoughts: 'My father wanted to make love to me from the moment I was born'; 'He keeps staring at my legs'; 'I'm afraid to be alone with him.' She then misidentified the author as her father, and was alternately erotic and hostile in manner. Rachael had concluded that the man who claimed he was her father could not be, and she was uncertain about the woman who said she was her mother. Rachael was really a princess but her real (royal) parents denied her existence.

In a calmer mood Rachael claimed that her husband deprived her of material comforts, left her alone at nights, was unfaithful, and when he did make love to her practised coitus interruptus, so leaving her unsatisfied. She hated him. Thus in this case an unsatisfying reality was replaced by the wish phantasy to have the former lover restored to her, and introversion of the libido had taken place, as in a hysterical neurosis. This was followed by regression to the sexual object of childhood – the father. Again, as in hysteria, the sexual wishes created anxiety and conflict. In contrast to hysteria, however, the conflict led to a break with reality: the unacceptable wishes were projected to the former lover and the father. The family romance phantasy served the same purpose, that of repudiating the incestuous wishes.

A contrast must be made between this type of case (a reactive psychosis), where there is the potential for a satisfying heterosexuality; and the other type, where fixations established in the course of development interfere with the ability to achieve libidinal satisfaction. But here too the turning to phantasy is also clear – as in the following case of a prostitution phantasy. Elsie

(Chapter 3) accused a woman neighbour, with whom she had previously been friendly, of drugging her and acting as a procuress; and of directing men to her house where they had coitus with her while under the influence of the drug. During the acute phase of the illness, Elsie frequently referred to homosexuality. She insisted that she heard other female patients talking about their homosexual practices.

As an adolescent Elsie had been sexually attracted to a girl with whom she worked, and had wished to be a boy so that they could make love. This homosexual love had forerunners in sexual games with other girls in childhood, and a close physical relationship with her mother. Indeed, her father's absence during the war enabled Elsie to share her mother's bed, and, using the excuse of the mother's ill health, she excluded him altogether. Only with the approach of her mother's death did Elsie leave the bed, and this at the age of 24. She had kept company with a young man, but gave him up after her mother's death; then at 29 she married another man but the marriage was a disappointment to her, and she blamed her husband for failing to satisfy her sexually.

The immediate cause of the illness was the visit of an American niece, who stayed with Elsie and her family. Although Elsie admired her niece she fell out with her, because she thought that the niece was putting (sexual) ideas into her son's head. Elsie was jealous, accusing her son of being more interested in the niece than in herself. But during the acute attack she expressed ideas indicating that the niece was in fact a homosexual love object – 'I have discovered I have the power to take over bodies and voices. I've taken my niece's body lots of times, I look at her and she becomes me.'

Elsie turned to phantasy to avoid the frustration of the sexual wish for her niece. Just as with the hysterical patient described earlier, the prostitution phantasy had the purpose of hiding the wish to act the part of the man in coitus with a woman. However, in the case of the psychotic patient this wish phantasy found conscious expression in a delusion. She believed that the men with whom she was forced to act the prostitute became part of

herself; the more so if they were men of importance and prominence. She said a leading politician came to her (coitus) and
became her –'I was the government', she claimed. The turning to
phantasy initiated a regression which highlighted the phallic-
masculine libido and its homosexual object (the mother). It also
led to a return to the incestuous love objects and to a re-enactment, through identification, of their act of coitus.

The problem of explanation

There is nothing new about the observations which have been
described here, and they can be made at any time. What,
however, is the explanation of the similarities between the
contents of the hysterical phantasies and the delusions of
psychotic patients? Do the phantasies expressed delusionally
reflect a mental development which, having reached the Oedipal
phase, then regressed – as in the hysterias – causing the incestuous wishes to suffer a change of aim and object? To most
psychoanalysts and psychiatrists it has seemed improbable that
the Oedipus phase could have been even precariously established in patients suffering from schizophrenic psychoses. For
the quality of their real object relations as they exist during the
illness and during the pre-psychotic period argues against such a
development ever having taken place.

This view gathered strength from therapeutic work by
psychoanalysts. When schizophrenic patients were engaged in
therapeutic ventures they presented a variety of phenomena,
amongst which were noted disorders of self/object discrimination, disturbances of object constancy, a pathological egocentrism and a tendency to externalize affects. All the resulting
manifestations – transitivism and appersonation, need-satisfying
behaviour, egocentrism and the externalization of hatred, envy
and jealousy – arose in relation to the analyst (Nunberg, 1921;
Bychowski, 1952: Hill, 1955; Pao, 1979). They did so under such
circumstances as to suggest that the various expressions of lack
of self/object discrimination reflected a continuing defence
against destructive wish phantasies (Rosenfeld 1954; Searles,

1963). Similarly the withdrawal, disinterest and inattention appeared to have the purpose, as did the sense of omnipotence, of defending against narcissistic injuries (Pao, 1979).

So striking were the sadistic wish phantasies, the anxieties and defences (splitting, projective identification) which could be discerned behind the repetitive phenomena emerging in treatment, that it seemed reasonable to assume that they must constitute the essence of the vulnerability to the illness. It was postulated that this complex of mental events must be in the nature of a repetition of a pathological infantile mental state. Once consolidated in these 'early times', it exerted its influence on succeeding phases of mental development. In turn phallic-Oedipal representations provided both means of representation for and a defence against the wish phantasies of the infantile psychopathological core (paranoid position, Rosenfeld, 1954; infantile autistic state, Searles, 1963). The phallic-Oedipal contents of delusional phantasies thus stood in relation to this core as the manifest content of a dream does to the latent dream thoughts.

From this standpoint the phallic-Oedipal contents can only be of secondary importance with respect to the psychopathological process. More specifically the envy, jealousy and anxieties which comprise the affective content of an Oedipal delusional phantasy are believed to be the result of a disturbed pre-Oedipal relationship with the mother (Blum, 1981; Meissner, 1978). The ensuing faulty regulation of narcissism thus created becomes the basis for the narcissistic quality of the delusional objects – those who are wished for and those who are persecutory (Pao, 1979). Again, the homosexual (phallic) anxiety so frequently represented in delusional phantasy is regarded as a defence against an oral-sadistic wish phantasy directed against the breast-penis, which, having been projected into the mother, is transformed into a dread of retribution (see Chapter 6). Finally, Oedipal rescue phantasy delusions are interpreted as the expression of an attempt to separate from the parent, and thus bring about the resolution of symbiotic relatedness with the mother (Searles, 1963).

At first sight it appears as if the phallic-Oedipal conflicts

PP-F

observable in the delusions of the schizophrenic patients cannot be accorded the pathogenic importance they undoubtedly have in hysterical neuroses. However, there are a number of observational as well as theoretical issues which must be considered before such a conclusion can be reached. It is well known that a variation exists, in the sphere of symptomatology and pre-illness personality, between cases of schizophrenic psychosis. There are those in which the ability to form close relationships outside the family has been severely impaired, while in others this is not so. It is rather in the former that the mental representations of instinct appear to have been stunted in their growth. Some would have it (see above) that this is because of the effect of primitive defences (splitting, projective identification, etc.) which have exerted a deleterious influence on the evolution of healthy (intrapsychic) object relationships. The personality is, therefore, deprived of the outlets necessary for the satisfaction of wishes and the resilience to meet frustrations, disappointments and object loss. Yet in these cases the onset of the illness occurs at a time when the patient is preoccupied with sexual phantasies and guilt about masturbation.

It is often in these cases that the delusional contents are of a sadistic nature. However, even in such instances it is possible to discern phallic-Oedipal phantasies and masturbatory guilt, hidden behind oral-sadistic phantasies. For example, Henry (see Chapter 2), who believed that his father was a murderer, complained about his upper left incisor tooth, fearing the pleasure he experienced when he touched the tooth with his tongue. It might cause him to bite someone, or even commit murder. When he was asked to expand on the dental sensations, he said that he could not resist pressing his tongue against his tooth – 'It gives me an interesting feeling, it charms me,' he said. 'It's something like a melodeon, a pushing in and out sort of feeling. It gets stiff and swollen. It's a bad habit and I must stop it.' His description strongly suggests that touching the tooth was a masturbatory equivalent, and that the tooth was not only a symbol of the penis but that the movement of tongue and tooth gave expression to a coital phantasy which he acted out when he bit his mother.

The fact that sadistic phantasies, as delusional contents, may serve to represent phallic-Oepidal wishes (see Bleuler, 1911) is in itself insufficient to contradict the view that antecedent (infantile) psychical events are primarily responsible for the predisposition to schizophrenic psychoses. However, there are cases of schizophrenia where the patient was able to establish a real, permanent heterosexual relationship. There are also the persecutory types of psychoses (paranoid psychoses, paranoid schizophrenia) where there was heterosexual object choice prior to the onset of the illness. These attacks are generally associated with a pre-existing state of frustration or disappointment. Were these patients able to proceed to heterosexual object choice because infantile experiences were less pathogenic, thus allowing a less restricted psychical development?

Available evidence from psychotherapeutic work does not support this hypothesis. The phenomena (transitivism, etc.) which are taken to reflect the existence of a pathogenic, infantile mental state are similar in patients who did proceed to object choice prior to the illness and in those who did not. Again, what significance is to be attached to the observation that these clinical manifestations (transitivism, etc.) are to be found entirely during acute attacks which arise at the onset of a schizophrenic or paranoid psychosis, or during its chronic course? Are these phenomena only non-specific consequences of the dissolution of psychical structures or are they, as it is claimed, the repetitive expression of the nucleus of the psychosis?

There is another, related problem, which also involves description and explanation. In both the schizophrenias and paranoid psychoses a turning from reality to phantasy (introversion) characterizes the initial stage of the illness. As far as hysterical neuroses are concerned, the phantasies are a revised and updated version of the incestuous object relationships of childhood. Symptom formation occurs when they become a danger which cannot be neutralized. At the onset of cases of schizophrenia an identical sequence of mental events can be traced out, but the outcome as far as symptomatology is concerned is different. Some delusional and hallucinatory contents indicate that, as in hysterical neuroses, early childhood experiences (fixations to objects and of instinct representations) have been revived by the turning from reality to phantasy. For instance, a young man (remitting schizophrenia) asserted that he was being sexually persecuted by a male friend, who, he believed, envied his manliness and success with women. In fact the young man's sexual life was confined to masturbation, but his heterosexual phantasies had recently been interrupted by disturbing homosexual images, and it was this that he accused his friend of causing. The patient had substituted a wish delusion of being handsome, attractive and successful with women in place of his disappointing and frustrating reality.

During the course of psychotherapy he reported that he was having evil thoughts, one being of the author's backside. He then had memories of his parents quarrelling, and heard noises he could not identify. Next he had a picture in his mind of his mother's buttocks and his father pushing his penis against her. Then he heard a girl's voice, and hoped this would prevent any homosexual thoughts coming to mind. The young man wanted to spit, because he believed that spit was the same as semen: if he spat the girl became pregnant and that would confirm his masculinity. This heterosexual phantasy facilitated the emergence of anxiety-provoking incestuous wishes, which had the following representation just after puberty. He had been in the habit of disposing of seminal fluid, after masturbation, by throwing it into a lavatory which was connected to a septic tank. But he came to fear that the semen would mix with his mother's and sister's menstrual blood, which he knew also ended up in the septic tank. He dreaded the periodic arrival of the men who came to empty the tank, lest they found dead infants inside. These frightening thoughts gave expression to the Oedipal wish to give his mother a child and to the wish to destroy any possible rivals in her womb, thought of as a cloaca.

In the remitting schizophrenias there is a return to reality *pari passu* with the remission of the illness. Otherwise there is a proliferation of delusional phantasies (non-remitting cases). Are the delusional phantasies of the remitting case similar to or different from those found in the long-standing chronic case? It may be that the controversy regarding the pathogenic significance of phallic-Oedipal conflicts has arisen because all types of persecutory psychoses, including the schizophrenias, are regarded as psychopathologically homogenous.

What evidence is there in favour of the idea that the delusional phantasies of the remitting cases are different in nature from those of non-remitting cases? Reference has already been made to a hypothesis based on innumerable observations (Bleuler, 1911; Tausk, 1919; Nunberg, 1921; Bychowski, 1952; Jacobson, 1954; Katan, 1979), that a primitive (primary, Freud, 1921) or psychotic form of identification underlies some of the most prominent symptoms which appear at the onset of schizophrenic and paranoid psychoses, irrespective of the courses these illnesses follow.

As described in Chapter 4, these psychotic identifications serve different purposes. They act as substitutes for object choices, as the expression of wish-fulfilment and as a means of defence (Freeman, 1985a). They are an integral element of the introversion to phantasy. Where identification replaces object choice after a lost love (Tausk, 1919), it has the effect of psychically restoring the love relationship. It fulfils the wish that the past become the present, the wish for a return to happy times. The persecutory experiences and appersonation are a consequence of the identification, subject to the hostile component of the ambivalent attitude to the lost object.

The turning to phantasy (introversion) is apparent when identification acts as wish-fulfilment. For instance, Derek (see Chapter 2) believed that Christ, in the guise of an astronaut, was returning to the world; as mentioned, he believed that he was to play an important part in this great undertaking. (Derek also claimed that he was married to a woman he had long admired but had been too timid to approach.) Although he later came to fear the astronauts as persecutors, he was simultaneously identified with them, as evidenced by certain bodily signs which he had in common with them. This man had found his life unsatisfying and lonely, and he spent much of his spare time reading books on astronomy and space flight; it was this material which provided the content of his delusions. In other cases the turning to phantasy is also to be found where identification has a defensive aim (Freeman, 1985a).

The clinical phenomena described in Chapter 4 suggest that the objects which comprise the content of delusions in chronic, non-remitting cases have an autonomy and a permanence, which sets them apart from the delusional objects of remitting cases. The influence of the former is such as to falsify the perception of real objects in an enduring manner, in contrast to the misidentifications of the remitting cases, which are generally transient. It is virtually impossible to establish connections of affective significance for the patient between the delusional objects and the object representations of the pre-psychotic phase. Thus great change has clearly taken place since the time of onset, when the psychotic identifications and the associated phantasies served the same purposes as those of the remitting cases. At this initial stage the delusional phantasies were the expression of a reaction to a disappointing and frustrating reality.

Clinical observation suggests that very frequently the delusional phantasies which appear in chronicity are no longer connected with those which occurred at the onset (see the cases of Edith, Sheila, Kath, Henry, Nettie, Ann, Christine and Geraldine). For example, Tom (Chapter 2) who said that he was to be awarded a large sum of money for services rendered to the hospital, did not have this delusion when he first fell ill – at that time the content of the psychotic attack consisted of homosexual and hypochondriacal fears. The wish delusion described made its appearance when, after a remission lasting some months, he fell ill again. The love object of the delusion was a girl he had only met a few times during the years prior to his illness. If it is true that these delusional phantasies only emerge later in the course of the psychosis, then, as suggested in Chapter 4, they are part of the psychical reconstruction which makes use of pre-existing pubertal and adolescent phantasies (Freud, 1924).

These delusional objects have no connection with the real objects of the pre-psychotic phase of the illness.

If all cases of schizophrenia and paranoid psychosis ended in full remission, or in a cyclical course without damage to the personality, it would not be unreasonable to conclude that, as in hysterical neuroses, phallic-Oedipal wishes cause the danger which leads to symptom formation, notwithstanding the psychical dissolution. However, this latter characteristic, and the fact that there are courses of illness which end in varying degrees of chronicity, have led to the alternative theory described above. It was then a short step to the assumption that this theory was explanatory for all cases, whatever their outcome. However, there are sufficient differences between the remitting and the non-remitting cases to indicate that such an assumption is hardly justified. What is common to all, however, are the ubiquitous phallic-Oedipal contents expressed directly or in a regressive form.

Why should these contents appear so consistently in individuals whose mental development has not reached that necessary for healthy and satisfying interpersonal relationships? Is it because the Oedipus complex evolves in the context of an inherited schema which, as Freud (1918) suggested, acts independently of the experience of the individual? Thus the male patient's wish to possess the mother as a love object creates castration anxiety, and regression to identification with the mother. The female patient fears retribution for death wishes against the mother, bringing about a regression from object choice (the father) to identification. The prevalence of passive feminine content in the delusions of male patients, and the derivatives of phallic sexuality expressed in the delusional ideas of female patients, are the result. The in-built Oedipal wish phantasies come to expression despite the multifarious forms of infantile and pre-Oedipal pathology which arise in those who succumb to paranoid and schizophrenic psychoses. Viewed in this way, the effect and the final expression of the schema (the Oedipus complex) would have the power to initiate the process of illness as they do in the neuroses. The causes of the psychical dissolution must lie in some special predisposition. It does not follow that this is formed as a result of a faulty infantile development.

CHAPTER 6

The delusion of persecution by a known person of the opposite sex

C RITICS of Freud's (1911) theory of persecutory paranoia cite as evidence of its falsity the delusion of persecution by a known member of the opposite sex. Persecutory paranoia – now commonly referred to as paranoid psychosis (Batchelor, 1964; Forrest, 1975) – can appear in the fourth decade of life, but is more frequently encountered in later years. A necessary condition for the diagnosis (Freud, 1911) is that prior to the onset of the illness the persecutor was well known to the patient: a friend or colleague. The delusion of persecution by the opposite sex seems to be confined to women. Where male patients complain of being persecuted by a woman, it emerges that the woman is only the agent of a male persecutor. The delusion of persecution of a woman by a man also occurs in remitting (schizophreniform) and non-remitting schizophrenias, where it is a transient phenomenon at the onset of the psychosis (see the cases of Kath and Hilda, Chapter 2). Usually the male persecutor is a teacher, public figure or someone known by sight.

The libidinal theory

According to Freud (1911), a friend or colleague becomes the object of homosexual love. In order to 'repress' this wish, a transformation of affect occurs: love is replaced by hate which is projected. Freud (1915b) refuted the criticism of his theory by showing, in the case of a female patient persecuted by a man, that an older woman could be identified as a homosexual love object. This is a commonly encountered situation: the patient has delusional ideas about two persons, a man and a woman, and the latter is the instigator of the plot.

A difficulty for the theory occurs in female cases where there is only a male persecutor. The persecutor is known but not necessarily well known – he may be the patient's doctor or dentist. The delusion may continue unaltered over many years without any serious disintegration of the remainder of the personality, and these cases usually occur during the last part of the third decade of life. They are often diagnosed as paranoid schizophrenia. Sometimes the onset is characterized by erotomania, and only later does the beloved become a persecutor (see the case of May, Chapter 2).

In reviewing Freud's (1915b, 1915c) contribution to the problem of the delusion of persecution by a member of the opposite sex, Katan (1974, 1979) expressed the view that Freud had overlooked the significance of the jealousy which is a part of the patient's delusional reality. In Freud's (1915b) case the patient believed that a love relationship existed between her homosexual love object and her persecutor. In the pre-psychotic phase, according to Katan (1974), jealousy led the patient to destroy this imagined relationship by making herself available to the man, thus using her heterosexuality in the service of her homosexuality. Her unconscious envy of the penis created a castration wish and the desire to act the part of the man with the homosexual love object, representing the mother.

A similar explanation is proposed for the female cases of paranoid schizophrenia where there is no sign of a female persecutor, and where the onset is characterized by erotomania (Freeman, 1984a). In these cases a symbolic representation of the love object is to be discerned. In his study of the patient described by Tausk (1919), and used by Freud (1915c) to illustrate the metapsychology of preconscious and unconscious thought processes, Katan (1979) suggested that the other woman (the third party) was symbolized by the church in which the patient's motor symptoms had occurred. The woman symbolized (the mother) was not a persecutor. She was, as in Freud's case (1915c), the object of the patient's homosexual desire. The patient was attracted to the heterosexual lover because he was substituted for the mother's penis. This the patient wished for herself so that she would act the part of the man in coitus.

The theory of the persecuting breast/mother

In Chapter 5 an account was given of the theories of those psychoanalysts who find it difficult to believe that illnesses as serious as paranoid psychosis and paranoid schizophrenia can be satisfactorily explained by concepts belonging to a sexual theory of neurosis. These theories are predicated on the belief that the danger which initiates the psychopathological process must be more menacing than that which leads to neurosis. Only a deadly danger could result in psychical dissolution and the consequences which this entails. Melanie Klein's work with neurotically disturbed young children revealed that they were oppressed by the most fearsome internal dangers long before they reach the phallic-Oedipal phase as described by Freud (1900). She was of the opinion (Klein, 1932) that the sadistic phantasies and fears of these children were '. . . identical with what, in adult paranoiacs, are known as delusions.'

Freud's homosexual theory of persecutory paranoia appeared to be further undermined by the existence of adult cases where persecutory delusions existed alongside an overt homosexuality. According to the libidinal theory, the homosexuality must be unconscious for the persecutory delusions to arise. If the homosexuality was conscious, how could it be the source of the persecutory delusions? In the course of the psychoanalytic treatment of these psychoses, where the homosexuality was overt, it appeared that when the patient felt threatened by his sadistic wish phantasies the homosexuality became more prominent (Rosenfeld, 1949). It was concluded that the homosexual wish discerned in the adult paranoiac patient acted as a defence against derivatives of the aggressive instinct.

It follows from the theories described in Chapter 5 that the persecutor in male and female cases of paranoid schizophrenia and paranoid psychosis is a substitute for part (the breast) or the whole mother endowed with attributes of the father (breast-penis; mother with the penis). The sadistic and acquisitive wish phantasies arising from envy (Klein, 1946) of the mother and the contents of her body (internalized penis, for example) are projected into the part or whole object to control or destroy it, and then introjected. The result is internal as well as external persecution. This hypothesis resolves the problem presented by the delusion of persecution of a woman by a man. The male persecutor is a substitute for the breast/mother/self.

The hypothesis of substitution by displacement (primary process) in paranoid psychoses and paranoid schizophrenia has its basis in the transference repetitions which occur during the psychoanalytic treatment of symptom and character neuroses. Where the analyst and the patient are male, the analyst may come to be treated and reacted to by the patient as if he were the mother: the patient can re-experience the anxiety once felt in his relationship with her. For example, a male patient, suffering from an anxiety hysteria, was unable to speak about his most personal thoughts because he feared the analyst's response would render him weak, helpless and unmanly. This had been his reaction when his mother criticized his utterances or behaviour, and he had put the male analyst in the place of a castrating pre-Oedipal mother. Similarly, female patients in treatment with a male analyst gave expression to mother transferences which may be an equal source of anxiety. Although male patients may also come to fear a female analyst in her mother transference role, they do not develop fixed persecutory delusions of the kind found in paranoid psychosis or in the paranoid type of schizophrenia (i.e. passivity experiences, delusional perceptions, etc.).

Assessment of the clinical phenomena

The concept of substitution is common to Katan's (1979) theory and to those collectively described here as the theory of the persecuting breast/mother. The concept of substitution enabled Katan (1979) to get round the problem presented by the delusion of persecution of a woman by a man where there is no female persecutor. A symbol substitutes for the mother, and the male persecutor for her penis. Those who subscribe to the theory of the persecuting breast/mother have no interest in seeking out a third (female) party, because the male persecutor represents the sadistic omnipotent (narcissistic) penis-breast mother. However, how does the substitution concept fare when a female persecutor is discovered subsequent to the patient's complaint of being persecuted by a man? In such cases the man cannot be a substitute for the woman, because he exists, but he is allocated a secondary role; the former is a separate and distinct entity from the latter as a mental representation.

An example is relevant here. A woman, aged 54, the wife of a soldier, complained that she was being persecuted by the colonel who commanded her husband's battalion. She accused him of causing her to experience genital sensations and inciting her neighbours to calumniate her as a prostitute. During several months in hospital she insisted on the reality of these experiences. Then one day she revealed that she had been worried about her husband's alcohol consumption, but had been comforted and reassured by her friend, a woman of her own age. The two had spent a lot of time together at the army depot until they were joined by another army wife, a woman some ten years younger. After this the patient no longer felt wanted by her friend and was unhappy. Then she became obsessed with the idea that the colonel wanted to get rid of her, and this was followed by the other delusional experiences. When trying to explain the colonel's motives to herself, she suddenly realized that it was the younger woman who was behind the plot. The woman had bribed the colonel with sexual favours to make her life unbearable and drive her mad. In this way the younger woman could have the patient's friend for herself. It is unnecessary here to enter into the psychopathological aspects of the illness, beyond pointing out that the immediate cause was the frustration caused by the husband's alcoholic impotence. However, the patient was jealous of her persecutor and she hated her, while the colonel was a substitute for a female persecutor, representing the mother or, as was more likely in this case, a sister.

Symptomatology provides yet further difficulties for theoretical constructions. From time to time female patients are encountered (see the case of Sheila, Chapter 2) whose illness begins with the delusion of being persecuted by a woman they have known well. After some time the female persecutor is replaced, wholly or in part, by a male persecutor. Thus Sheila complained, at first, of being slandered by an older woman she knew at work; after some months this delusion receded, and she began to hear a man's voice, using foul and obscene words. He threatened to rape her and split her up the middle, and he accused her of soiling her bed masturbating. In another female patient (see the case of May, Chapter 2), the voice of a male persecutor was replaced by that of her father, equally insulting and disparaging.

Lastly, there is the problem of the relationship between the fixed delusions of the paranoid psychoses and the paranoid type of schizophrenia, and the transient delusion of persecution by a man in young female patients between the ages of 14 and 22 and experienced at the onset of the illness. In these cases there is either a remission of the illness or a gradual movement towards chronicity (moderate or moderately severe end state).

The theory that the male persecutor in female cases of paranoid psychosis and paranoid schizophrenia is a substitute for a woman (the breast/mother suffused with sadism emanating from parts of the self) must be seriously questioned in view of the clinical phenomena just described. The male persecutor cannot be regarded as substituting for a woman in view of his existence as a mental representation distinct from the representation of a female figure (persecuting or non-persecuting). How is the theory to be reconciled with those cases where the female persecutor is replaced by a male persecutor?

The problems provoked by the clinical phenomena can be

resolved by turning to the idea that the male persecutor represents, through externalization, the patient's wished-for masculinity. Simultaneously, this narcissistic object acts as a
repository, through projection, of masturbatory excitement. As
described in Chapter 4 (see the case of Emma), it is not
uncommon to encounter female patients who accuse their male
persecutor of being inflamed with sexual passion and having to
give way to masturbation. This excitement has as its ideational
counterpart a sadistic castration phantasy. Then, too, the change
from a female to a male persecutor which occurs in some patients
can also be accommodated into the above-mentioned
hypothesis. Initially the female persecutor is a superego figure
reacting against the masculine, acquisitive wishes, hence the
patient's belief that she is slandered and maligned. With the
increasing weakening of the ego the sadistic, phallic sexuality is
projected along with the externalization of the wished-for
masculinity. The persecutor now gives expression to the
patient's phallic sadism. This hypothesis also draws together the
delusion of persecution of a woman by a man as it occurs in
adolescent schizophrenias, the paranoid type of schizophrenia
and paranoid psychosis. The disappearance of the delusion in
the adolescent schizophrenias is accounted for in terms of the
continuing dissolution of psychical structures.

The weakness of the theory of substitution must also hold for
male paranoiac patients, who complain of being persecuted by a
known member of their own sex. The male patient really fears a
man, not a woman. Why do women not appear as principal
persecutors in male cases? Perhaps this question can best be
answered by first pointing to the envy which characterizes
female patients who complain of persecution by a man. These
women are envious of the penis and cannot rid themselves of a
castration wish phantasy. Their persecutory fears are due to
dread of a man's revenge. The absence of female persecutors in
male cases indicates that the man does not fear revenge at the
hands of a woman. Men may fear woman for many reasons and
this can be traced to fear of the mother. The homosexual fears
his mother's castrated state and identifies with her as a phallic

being. Male paranoiacs retain their heterosexuality, either in phantasy or in reality, and they almost always deny a homosexual interest. Despite this, however, they are frequently fearful that others might regard them as homosexuals. What is the source of their fear? Freud (1911) drew attention to the necessity of distinguishing between the sexual deviation, homosexuality and unconscious homosexuality (see also Frosch, 1983). The clinical phenomena of paranoid psychoses favour Freud's view that the persecutory fears of the male patient derive from unconscious homosexuality: the male patient either dreads being used sexually as a woman by the unconsciously loved man, or he dreads retribution for his envy and wish to possess the loved man's penis. Unlike the homosexual, he does not unconsciously wish to play the part of the phallic mother with a male lover representing himself or vice versa. The overt homosexuality which is present in a small number of male patients with persecutory delusions must, therefore, be regarded as having a completely different origin from the unconscious homosexuality which leads to the delusional ideas.

The clinical and psychopathological data presented here support the concept of a primary penis envy in women. Only the presence of such an envy can explain why certain women complain of persecution by a man. If an equivalent envy – for example, of the breast or of pregnancy – existed in men then the delusion of persecution of a man by a woman should occur. The pre-Oedipal boy may well envy his mother's capacity to bear children. However, once he becomes aware of the female's lack of a penis (i.e. when he reaches the phallic-Oedipal phase) he no longer envies the woman. This is the reason why the delusion of persecution of a man by a woman is not to be found in male patients suffering from any of the persecutory types of psychosis.

CHAPTER 7

Psychoanalytic aspects of organic mental states

THE DISORDERS of mental life which are caused by physical diseases, alcohol and drugs can be a rich source of knowledge and experience for the psychoanalyst working in the mental hospital. An earlier generation of psychoanalysts involved themselves in the study and treatment of these conditions. Betlheim and Hartmann's (1924) investigation into Korsakov's psychosis, Hollos and Ferenczi's (1925) study of general paresis and Hoffer's (1955) report on a case of post-encephalitis lethargica are instances of these endeavours.

Today there are no longer the large numbers of patients suffering from these conditions, and their place has been taken by cases of senile dementia and cerebral arteriosclerosis. The treatment of these conditions, and of the other chronic brain syndromes (Pick's disease, Alzheimer's disease and Huntington's chorea), provides an opportunity for study from the psychoanalytic point of view.

In acute and chronic brain syndromes the dissolution of the ego has two consequences. It leads to the expression of wish phantasies and to specific modes of mental functioning which make adaptation to reality impossible. As to the former, the psychical fulfilment of wishes does not necessarily lead to pleasure and contentment: anxiety is often intense, suggesting that their presence has resulted in conflict. This in turn suggests that in such instances the ego and superego have not been completely inactivated. A 50-year-old woman, for example, strained her back, and was given a simple analgesic. As there was no improvement pentazocine was prescribed every four hours, and about twenty-four hours later she became delirious, saying that her husband and her best (woman) friend were dead. She was hallucinated: voices told her that she was to be killed because she had been unfaithful to her husband. She was panic stricken.

Unknown to the doctor who had prescribed the pentazocine, the patient had for a long time been drinking at least half a bottle of whiskey a day. The delirium had been a response to the combination of alcohol and pentazocine, and an explanation of its content was soon forthcoming. The patient's husband had been impotent for several years, and she had latterly turned to alcohol to deaden her sexual desires. At an earlier time she had been unfaithful on a few isolated occasions. In the delusion her preconscious sexual wishes for her husband's friend were about to be fulfilled; her death wishes against his wife equally so. However, due to the psychical dissolution the conflict which had existed preconsciously between her wishes and the superego was externalized in so far as the latter constituted the content of the hallucinations.

From studies on the oculogyric signs of encephalitis lethargica, Jelliffe (1932) concluded that, as in the case just described, the upsurge of wish phantasies leads to conflict because of their unacceptability to the remainder of the personality. Under such conditions there develop self-reproach, depression of mood and bouts of anxiety and agitation. Stengel (1930, 1935) also suggested that the obsessive-compulsive phenomena which occur in post-encephalitic cases can be regarded as a reaction and a defence against destructive, aggressive impulses released by the disease process. However, in other cases of encephalitis, as in acute and chronic brain syndrome, no regressive-like symptoms appear, although there may be destructive outbursts and hyperactivity (Schilder, 1951). It is to be presumed that in these instances the superego has succumbed to a widespread dissolution of psychical structure. The liberated drive derivatives, unacceptable to conscience and controlled in the healthy state, do not provoke conflict nor lead to symptoms through compromise. This is most strikingly encountered in cerebral diseases, such as Pick's disease and some cerebral tumours, which follow a deteriorating course. Sublimations and reaction formations are gradually undermined with the patient finding pleasure in all forms of auto-erotic activity (Freeman, 1969).

In his writings on organic psychoses, Schilder (1976a) drew attention to other psychoanalytic writers who were inclined to ignore what he described as defect symptoms or, in Jacksonian terms, negative symptoms. Judgement, memory and perception were impaired in diffuse cerebral degenerations. These losses of function had the effect of heightening suggestibility, promoting egocentrism, encouraging confabulations and blurring the distinction between wishful thinking and reality considerations. It was Schilder's opinion (1976b) that in organic psychoses the morbid process did not affect the core of the personality, but was limited to the 'perceptive ego' (Schilder, 1924). Thus the wishful thinking, the condensations and displacements (primary process) which affected verbal ideas acted on impersonal data alone. The primary process was therefore limited to conscious and preconscious thoughts.

These formulations (Schilder, 1951, 1976a) derived from observations made on general paresis, aphasias and agnosias are apposite for the majority of cases of arteriosclerotic, pre-senile and senile dementias. The 'defect' or negative symptoms can be clearly observed when regular meetings are held, particularly with cases of the amnesic syndrome, the majority of which are due to cerebral arteriosclerosis. Here the 'defect' is limited to the loss of short-term memory, loss of time sense and judgement. Otherwise speech and control of motility are preserved. Patients of this type can engage in lively conversation, even though they may forget within seconds what they were talking about.

In a group these patients show an interest in one another, but the self-centredness which Schilder (1976a) describes is much in evidence. They are handicapped by the difficulty of remembering each other's names or the name of the psychiatrist. In fact the name presents less difficulty than recall of his occupation (doctor): after a few meetings his name is recalled quite easily, but even after many months of regularly held meetings they cannot address the psychiatrist as doctor. The functional element ('repression') would appear to be of significance here. At best patients identify the doctor in terms of their own previous occupation, and this suggests that the verbal representations of self and other are no longer clearly differentiated.

In many cases, and especially in senile dementia, the patient does not wholly acknowledge the reality of his immediate environment. He forgets the name of the hospital, however often it is mentioned in discussion. He will insist that he is at home or at work, and the past is alive in everything he says. External impressions are altered to fit into his reality. For instance, one woman, suffering from attacks, saw smoke coming from the hospital chimney. Immediately she said, 'There's the old mill – Dinsmore's.' She was in fact referring to the mill near her home, where she had lived for many years.

This wishful thinking is strengthened by the misidentifications which occur despite the retention of a relatively intact cognition, apart from the defect of short-term memory. In group meetings patients address others as workmates, brothers or sisters, while misidentifying nurses as sister or mother and doctors as brother or father. These misidentifications are different from those which occur in acute brain syndromes, and they show the extent to which the present has become the past. All these phenomena follow from the action of the primary process. Regularly held meetings with these patients have the effect of strengthening the patient's awareness of reality by the correction of his misperceptions by others in the group. The regressive movement, facilitated by the injury to perception and memory – Schilder's 'perceptual ego' – is temporarily halted.

In arteriosclerotic and senile dementias it is the preconscious representation of objects that is disorganized, not their role as recipients of object cathexis. This is borne out by the fact that when the correct word or name is not available to the patient, he finds other verbal representations with which the correct one is associated (paraphasias and periphrasis). It indicates that cathexes are constantly attempting to invest object representations, and the behaviour of patients with others shows this to be true. Object cathexis is not abandoned, and it may be inferred from, for example, the misidentifications that the object representations in the system unconscious are intact and cathected.

These observations offer insight into the relationship which exists between size, shape and distance (perceptual) constancies and object constancy (the maintenance of object cathexis). Perceptual constancies can be extensively disorganized and yet object constancy remains intact. Object cathexis continues in existence even though there is no longer a stable preconscious representation of the object. This supports the view that '. . . the two processes (perceptual constancy and object constancy) are different from each other' (Freud, A., 1968).

The defect of memory and the falsification of reality in arteriosclerotic dementia cannot wholly be attributed to the loss of the function of attention, in its active and selective aspects, despite evidence of mental registration of auditory percepts. Neither is it simply a matter of denial, although it is clear that the falsification of reality allows external events of a distressing nature (being in hospital, etc.) to be excluded from consciousness. Denial deprives the perceptual data from obtaining the cathexis required for consciousness. These decathected representations of reality are replaced by preconscious wish phantasies, which are of a type common to all patients, and in this respect do not trench upon specific elements in the personality as Schilder (1976a) described. These non-specific wishes – to be young, active, at home with spouse and children – are fulfilled, as are wishes to be reunited with parents long since deceased. The expression of these wishes in hallucinatory form (Freud, 1900) falsifies the perception of reality and those in it. There are misidentifications and an alteration of overheard speech in terms of the wish-fulfilments.

In the schizophrenias, misidentification, hallucinations, memory lapses and disorders of speech form also occur; a decathexis of the system preconscious has also taken place here. As in organic mental states the decathected ideas become the vehicle for wishes: these are of a nature specific for the individual personality, but are no less affected by the primary process, hence the misidentifications and hallucinations. This apart, the significant difference between schizophrenias and organic psychoses of the kind described lies in the fact that in the latter it is the system preconscious which is primarily affected. In the schizophrenias the disturbance traverses the whole of the mental apparatus. There is a wholesale decathexis of all forms of representation, including those in the system unconscious – it is this which leads to the loss of object constancy.

Delusions and hallucinations with a persecutory content may also be a feature of the chronic brain syndrome. In arteriosclerotic and senile dementias they may arise within the context of an acute exacerbation when there is heightened confusion; ephemerally at night, or as a constant feature of the condition. When it is possible to obtain fuller information from the patient, it becomes clear that the origin of the paranoid symptom complex lies in conflicts which have been activated or exposed by the effect of the morbid process. These conflicts may or may not have had a pathological expression in the pre-illness period (i.e. prior to the dementia), either in the form of neurotic symptomatology, or in the shape of character traits (e.g. suspiciousness, pronounced envy or jealousy).

The occurrence of paranoid symptom complexes in organic mental states indicates that the morbid process has affected more than the perceptive ego (Schilder, 1976a). As long as repression remains operative there is neither consciousness of unacceptable wish phantasies, nor awareness of the latter as ego-alien experiences (obsessions, ideas of reference, etc.). The delusions are not simply the result of the loss of self/object discrimination, because such a loss is commonplace in cases of senile dementia where delusions of persecution are absent. Where they exist it is reasonable to assume, first, that psychical dissolution has led to the 'release' of unacceptable wish phantasies; and, second, that less advanced defences – externalization, denial and projection – have taken the place of repression, which has been subject to injury.

Some support for this explanation of delusional and hallucinatory manifestations in cerebral diseases is provided by those cases which present initially as 'functional psychoses'. It is not uncommon to encounter what, at first sight, appears to be a case of paranoid psychosis. For example, an elderly woman complains that her neighbours are gossiping about her. They say that she had led a life of promiscuity and should be shunned by everyone. In other cases, unknown persons are entering the patient's house in order to obtain evidence of a criminal act they believe the latter has committed. In some of these cases there is evidence of essential hypertension or ischaemic heart disease. Nevertheless, at the time of admission to hospital short-term memory and other cognitive functions are intact. Six months or a year later the patient is readmitted to hospital, showing signs of the beginning of a 'dementing' process; the persecutory phenomena may or may not have returned. Sometimes the immediate cause of these 'organic' psychoses is easy to discover and it is easy to observe how the psychical consequences of the cerebral disease have formed the content of the persecutory delusions.

A case in point is that of a widow, aged 65. Her complaint was of the kind described above: neighbours were saying that she invited men to come to the house to have sexual intercourse. She found herself experiencing genital sensations which, to her mind, were being induced by unknown persecutors. On physical examination she was found to be suffering from ischaemic heart disease, but there were no signs of cardiac failure. Her cognitive functions were intact, and a diagnosis of paranoid psychosis was made. It appeared that her husband, who had died a year previously, was her second: she had left her first when she was 35 and took up with the man who was to become her second. The first marriage had been unsatisfactory to her in all respects, and she longed for the closeness and intimacy which she and her second husband had enjoyed. After his death she had been disturbed by sexual need and had on one or more occasions given way to masturbation; however, guilt ended this practice and the sexual desire disappeared. The patient's symptoms rapidly responded to modest doses of phenothiazines, but about a year later she was readmitted to hospital because of failing short-term memory following a transient cerebral ischaemic attack. The delusional ideas had returned, and a diagnosis of arteriosclerotic dementia was made.

In this case there is reason to believe that the organic (cerebrovascular) process was active prior to and during the seemingly functional psychotic attack. If so, it must have affected the ego organization (dissolution limited in extent), causing a weakness in the repression mechanism. This wish for a man to satisfy her in the manner which led her to be unfaithful to her first husband could neither be fulfilled in reality, nor repressed successfully. The revulsion against masturbation, caused no doubt by accompanying conscious or unconscious phantasies, led at first to a superego reaction. The psychical dissolution was such as to lead to an externalization of the superego, and then to projection of the masturbatory excitement.

Elements of the patient's personality were exposed, as in a functional psychosis, but here the cause was organic in nature. If it is true that it was the disease process, clinically latent, which led to the psychical dissolution and to delusion formation, then it is not necessarily correct, as Schilder (1951) believed, that in organic mental states the morbid process must necessarily begin in the periphery – as in aphasias and apraxias – and proceed centripetally to the core of the personality. It is possible that, under certain conditions, the morbid process initially affects the core of the personality and then moves centrifugally, as postulated by Schilder for psychogenic disorders.

The investigation of cerebral diseases, from the clinical standpoint, also affords the opportunity of observing at first hand aspects of mental life which can only be inferred from the study of the mentally healthy, and those suffering from neuroses and personality problems. Repetitive phenomena may be taken as illustrative of this process. Perseverative phenomena, for example, are to be found in a wide range of pathological states: in senile and pre-senile dementia, in epileptic states, in cerebral arteriosclerosis, in brain tumour and after cerebral trauma. To this list can be added cerebral anoxia from whatever cause, and focal lesions due to vascular accidents resulting in asphasias, apraxias and mental defect.

A number of writers have already drawn attention to the fact that two distinct forms of perseveration can be distinguished (Goldstein, 1943; Luria, 1965). The first consists of the repetition of an action, which ceases only when a new stimulus is given to the patient; the second comprises an inability to abandon the reaction to a stimulus, even when a new one is presented. The former has been termed 'compulsive repetition' and the latter 'impairment of switching' (Luria, 1965).

Perseverative phenomena of both kinds are to be found in all the conditions referred to above, although it would appear that 'compulsive repetition' may preponderate in one clinical category, while 'impairment of switching' may be more frequent in another. This was found to be so when the incidence of the two types of perseveration was assessed in chronic schizophrenic states and in organic dementia (Freeman and Gathercole, 1966). These phenomena are also rarely encountered in isolation. Most often they are accompanied by defects in short-term memory with accompanying confabulations, by disturbances in orientation (again due to memory defect) with added misidentifications leading to a disorientation for place and person. Topographic memory and memory for names of body parts are sometimes defective also.

In these various clinical states, perseveration may appear in speech, thinking, motor and sensory functions. As well as being unable to terminate a motor act ('compulsive repetition'), or initiate a new one when the appropriate stimulus is presented ('impairment of switching'), a patient may continue to localize a stimulus to the hand when the stimulus has been transferred to the cheek. Critchley (1964) has described this type of sensory perseveration as a manifestation of parietal lobe disease, but it can also be observed in diffuse cerebral disease.

Focal cerebral lesions which lead to aphasias and apraxias provide abundant evidences of perseveration in speech and in behaviour. In these conditions, however, the gross memory defect, the misidentification and confabulations which characterize the other conditions are usually absent. It is of course likely that in the early stages of a degenerative cerebral condition, perseverative signs may appear without major alterations in memory and consciousness, as they seem to do in the dysphasias. It would be inadmissible to maintain that perseverative phenomena only appear coincidentally with a major deterioration of cognitive functions (Allison, 1962).

Before beginning a discussion of the mechanisms which may underlie perseverative signs, it is necessary to describe some observations which can be made during their occurrence. In the case of 'compulsive repetition' the reaction continues indefinitely and inappropriately until a new stimulus is presented. In the case of an 'impairment of switching' the patient is apparently unable to respond to the second stimulus. Stimulus 1 is followed by reaction 1; stimulus 2 by reaction 1; stimulus 2 again by reaction 1. Unlike 'compulsive repetition', 'failure of switching' involves the operation of a second stimulus, and the reaction does not continue indefinitely. In the case of sensory perseveration (see above), the switching defect can be brought to an end if the second stimulus is made sufficiently strong.

Several inferences can be drawn from these observations which may help to identify the mental functions involved in the expression of these phenomena. In the phenomenon of compulsive repetition it seems at first as if there is a defect in the mechanism that should terminate the response (failure of inhibition). Yet this mechanism must be intact, since it can be activated by external stimulus. This suggests that the defect may lie in the processes which release the inhibitory mechanism.

In the case of 'impairment of switching' a second stimulus does not bring the first response to an end, and neither does it lead to the correct reaction. This happens only if the second stimulus is sufficiently intense. A single explanation for both phenomena is available if it is assumed that the area of dysfunction involves the sphere of consciousness which subserves purposive attention.

A further category of repetitive manifestations – echo phenomena – are to be found in a wide range of pathological conditions. They occur in aphasias, in mental defect, in dementias and in schizophrenic psychoses; two main forms are usually described – in speech (echolalia), and in motor behaviour (echopraxia). They bear a striking resemblance to perseverations in that there is a common element of repetition. It is pronounced in echolalia, where the stimulus words are repeated over and over again without any regard for the context within which they appear. Echopraxia is rather different in that the action copied ceases whenever a new perceptual stimulus is presented to the patient. Even here, however, the compulsive character of the action reveals itself in the patient's apparent inability to stop the motor behaviour.

It is worth recalling that echo reactions (echopraxia) can be observed in healthy individuals when they are talking together in a face to face situation. At different times each assumes a posture or mannerism adopted by the other, and neither party is conscious of the fact that the movement has been initiated by a stimulus emanating from his companion. Awareness of the perceptual stimulus either limits or terminates what was, until that moment, a compulsive action undertaken outside consciousness. In this respect there is a similarity to the echopraxia of the sick individual who can, but only with difficulty bring his motor behaviour to an end with the aid of a new stimulus provided by the physician.

The data suggest that just as with perseverative signs, an explanation of echo reactions cannot be undertaken without reference to the condition of consciousness obtaining in the patient. The fact that emphasis is laid here on the role of consciousness does not in any way contradict those hypotheses which regard echo reactions as either the result of a perceptual dysfunction (Chapman and McGhie, 1964) or as the expression of a failure in self/object discrimination (Stengel, 1947). Both of these formulations propose a disturbance in cognition which must have as its consequence a derangement of consciousness.

Traumatic dreams, which comprise the third category of repetitive phenomena, have a much greater organizational complexity than either perseveration or echo reaction. These dreams are characterized by a repetitiveness which distinguishes them from all others except the less common recurrent dream occasionally reported by patients. It is this characteristic repetition which provides common ground with perseverations and echo phenomena. Like other dreams, the traumatic dream is essentially a visual perceptual experience, self-centred and therefore tending towards the concrete. These dreams are invariably accompanied by a distressing anxiety which may lessen in intensity with the passage of time.

It is now recognized that the mental state obtaining at the time of an experience is what determines whether or not the experience will be traumatic. Thus the anxious expectation almost universally present in combatant soldiers renders them prone to psychological traumatization. Traumatic dreams are usually a feature of a traumatic neurosis which has as its other symptoms mental tension, somatic signs of anxiety, headache, an inability to tolerate noise, and irritability. It is uncommon to find such a patient preoccupied with the traumatic experience or easily able to recall the details of the event. Hence the re-experiencing of the trauma in sleep is thus in striking contrast to the circumstances of the waking state. The dream proceeds in a state of consciousness which is different from that of wakefulness. Has the state of consciousness obtaining during dreaming a bearing on the problem of why traumatic dreams are repetitive?

The fourth group of clinical phenomena which also have a repetitive nature is best observed in the course of psychoanalytic treatment. A simple example is provided by the patient who finds it difficult to accept that his thoughts will be received sympathetically. He often behaves as if the opposite were the case, and it soon transpires that he has transferred on to the therapist feelings which once were directed towards a feared teacher at school. A more subtle expression of a similar trend is one where a patient finds it hard to speak, there having been no difficulty earlier. This pattern of behaviour only becomes comprehensible when it is understood that a stubborn silence was the way in which the patient acted towards his father when they had disagreed.

The compulsive element in the repetition of earlier behavioural patterns is most strikingly demonstrated in the phenomenon described as 'acting out in the transference' (Freud, 1914a). Instead of recalling a particular memory or series of memories, the patient behaves in specific ways either inside or outside the consulting room. The example of difficulty in speaking would be an instance of the former; in just the same way, the silence of another patient represents the compulsive repetition of times in childhood where she sat silently and happily at her father's feet. The latter type of 'acting out in the transference' is illustrated by the patient who involves wife or husband in a controversy over the benefits of treatment or provokes the spouse to criticism of the analyst. The fictitious conflict set up in the patient's mind between spouse and analyst eventually turns out to be a re-enactment of the continuous parental discord which characterized the patient's childhood.

Reference must also be made to the compulsive repetition of childhood sexuality which invariably occurs in the psycho-analysis of sexual deviations. These periods of 'acting out in the transference', which consist of bouts of deviant behaviour, are often stimulated by disappointments in the analyst, either because of breaks in the treatment or by some unreasonable expectation which is not met. Further analysis always shows that both the expectations and the disappointments which provide the stimulus for the compulsive reaction – the acting out – are repetitions of traumatic childhood experiences.

A further illustration of the operation of compulsive and repetitive trends in highly organized mental functions is again provided by the psychoanalytic treatment situation. Here the means of defending against unwanted wishes or against conscience are automatic, repetitive and outside consciousness. Projective mechanisms utilized in early life to deal with sexual or aggressive drives are also set in motion in the treatment situation under appropriate endopsychic stimulation. A similar situation is encountered with repression, denial or introjection: the patient fails to recognize that he is reacting to a stimulus in a stereotyped and mechanical manner and that his reaction is no longer appropriate.

In all clinical categories described, a special relationship exists between the phenomena and consciousness. In the case of perseverations and echo reactions, the cognitive status of the individual patient is defective in one or more functions. Memory defects leading to amnesias of different kinds, faulty registration and recall of immediate events, and reactive confabulations and misidentifications result in disorientation for place and person. In these conditions, therefore, a state of consciousness far removed from that necessary for environmental adaptation is present. The observable facts suggest that in both types of perseveration the defect in consciousness centres around the function of attending. In 'compulsive repetition' attention is only activated by the presentation of a strong stimulus. This alone appears to carry with it an inhibition of the repetitive behaviour.

The situation obtaining when 'impairment of switching' occurs also appears to involve attending. The ability to respond appropriately to a second stimulus only arises when the latter is sufficiently strong. This indicates once again that active attention, with the concomitant stimuli, is faulty, and that adequate functioning will be restored only when the stimulus becomes sufficiently intense to attract the impaired attention to itself. A defect of consciousness seems to be implicated also in those individuals who present with echo reactions. Here the manifestations – particularly the motor reactions – can be brought to a halt by helping the patient to direct his attention to them.

The traumatic dream presents a different problem in that there is no apparent damage to cognitive functions. The patient experiences the dream through a state of consciousness different from that of waking life. For in dreams attention is characterized by a passivity, and it is attracted by ideational contents and imagery which have the most vivid sensory intensity. The revival of the trauma takes place apart from the patient's will and certainly not at his command. Its presence is only possible in consequence of the state in sleep and the altered state of consciousness which characterizes dreaming.

Under normal circumstances purposive attention has a mobile quality, and in the very act of attending there is a restricting and inhibiting influence on extraneous or immediately past stimulation. It would seem that in a variety of organic brain disorders, and in some schizophrenic psychoses, the processes underlying attending are disorganized, thus leading, in part at any rate, to the perseverations and echo phenomena.

Perseverations and echo phenomena, as mentioned, occur outside awareness, and they are both repetitive and compulsive in quality. Transference phenomena which arise in the treatment of the neuroses differ from the three categories thus far described in so far as cognition is intact and the individual is in the waking state. Nevertheless, the behavioural patterns exhibited occur unconsciously. The patient has no awareness of the automatic nature of his reactions, or of the fact that he is without free will when presented with certain stimuli. In this respect he is no different from the patient who exhibits perseveration of the compulsive repetition variety.

The neurotic patient also exhibits an 'impairment of switching', and it is this which causes him to continue to react inappropriately in spite of interpretation and extensive 'working through'. It is this inability to abandon old and disadvantageous patterns of reacting which gives the impression that the mental function of some patients is characterized by a rigidity which opposes change. The psychoneurotic patient has no more control of his reactions than has the senile patient who cannot bring a motor act to an end. This control becomes a possibility for the psychoneurotic patient only when his attention is drawn to the repetitive and compulsive behaviour.

It is the task of the psychoanalyst to direct the patient's attention to mental contents and behaviour which up until this time have been unconscious; this is achieved by description and interpretation. As far as the patient is concerned it requires that his attentive capacity is mobile and freely available for deployment to whatever area is indicated by the analyst's interventions. Without such an efficiently functioning attentive process analytic therapy becomes impossible.

In the neuroses psychological factors (resistances) periodically impede the free movement of attention, and prevent the patient from recognizing the compulsive and repetitive nature of his thinking, affect and behaviour when confronted with specific stimuli. In organic mental states, and in some schizophrenic reactions, attention has lost its adaptational function because of damage to cerebral structures. Simple and uncomplicated repetitive behaviour can be terminated in these organic reactions through vigorous stimulation, but such correction becomes impossible when mental functions which subserve abstract thinking are involved. The damage to the attentive function has been too great and thus cannot be employed to give insight.

Thus far no mention has been made of those pathological conditions in which a defect of attention constitutes one of the major clinical manifestations. For the most part, these phenomena of inattention cannot be accounted for on the basis of lesions of the peripheral (sensory) nervous system. They may appear on the level of sensation, in visual or auditory perception, and even in the sphere of conceptualization. The faulty functioning can therefore manifest itself at either the most simple or at the most complex level of mental organization in just the same way as compulsive and repetitive phenomena.

In the case of tactile inattention, Allison (1962) has stated that the phenomenon was mostly seen in patients in whom there is either a slight clouding of consciousness or minimal sensory impairment. The inattention occurred most commonly in patients suffering from focal vascular or neoplastic lesions affecting the parietal area of the brain. Allison also noted that as the level of consciousness rose the inattention disappeared.

A more complex form of inattention is represented by the syndrome of anosognosia, where there is non-perception of physical defects. Although there are cases – usually of left hemiplegia – in which orientation, speech and memory appear to be intact, it is more common to find anosognosia associated with severe cognitive disorganization. On the basis of a study of twenty-two cases of cerebral disease, Weinstein and Kahn (1950) have proposed that the non-perception is always an aspect of a generalized disturbance of behaviour characterized by amnesias, confabulations, disorientation, paraphasias and perseverative signs.

In some chronic schizophrenic states, a series of phenomena can be observed not unlike the cases of organic non-perception. Here speech and thinking defects may make identification of the patient's communications difficult, but it is usually possible to note a restriction of attention which expresses itself in a denial of all or parts of their bodies. Such patients insist that their bodily movements or functions are foreign, and must therefore belong to the body of some other person. Usually these patients misidentify to such an extent that they do not acknowledge the nurses and doctors as nurses and doctors, or the hospital as a hospital. Tactile inattention can also be demonstrated. As in the case of patients demonstrating the syndrome of anosognosia (Weinstein and Kahn, 1950), this form of inattention is part of a wider symptom complex in which are to be found amnesias, confabulations, perseverative signs and echo phenomena as well as misidentifications.

It would appear, therefore, that repetitive phenomena are usually associated with extensive cognitive dysfunctions, an essential component of which is a faulty active attending. At the same time, repetitive phenomena on a more advanced level of mental organization also occur, but here the major dysfunction does not consist of a cognitive disorganization but of an inability to utilize attention in such a way as to bring under control of consciousness inappropriate and compulsive thinking, feeling and behaving. It is this latter type of repetitive phenomena which can be observed most easily in the transference behaviour of psychoneurotic patients.

In organic states the perseverative signs and echo phenomena are positive signs, in the Jacksonian sense, and represent the emergence of a primitive type of mental functioning. Transference phenomena can be thought of in the same way, except that their expression is less direct. Transferences, however, are no less automatic and no more under control than the less complicated sensori-motor phenomena. Unless identified, they can be mistakenly regarded as just another aspect of consciously directed thinking and behaving.

The importance of perseverative phenomena for a more direct approach to the understanding of the nature of psychological processes did not escape Schilder (1924), who recognized that they had a far-reaching significance for general psychology. He pointed out that these phenomena indicate, in the clearest possible fashion, a basic law of mental functioning – namely, that an impression is not utterly obliterated when it fades from consciousness, but that what once existed tends to re-emerge. Thus according to him, 'The influence of preceding impressions, the tenacity of retention, their after-effects in general, are basic psychophysical phenomena . . .'

It was only a short step for Schilder to recognize that Freud's (1920) concept of repetition compulsion, derived from the study of dreams and transference behaviour, described the expression of the same repetitive and compulsive principle. The tendency of mental processes to continue in the same functional pattern was again referred to by Freud (1916) when he stated that one of the greatest obstacles standing in the way of altering the course of thinking and feeling was an 'adhesiveness of the libido'. He meant by this that once libidinal cathexes had attached themselves to an object, disengagement became extremely difficult, if not impossible. Freud also believed that the degree of such 'adhesiveness' varied from one individual to the next, and that this was an independent factor which played a most important part in the aetiology of the neuroses. There seems every reason to believe that this inability to relinquish a pattern of thinking or behaving, even though it has become distinctly disadvantageous and inappropriate, can only result from the influence of a compulsive repetition inherent in mental activity.

The treatment of a psychoneurotic patient by psychoanalysis, or by a non-directive form of psychotherapy, leaves the therapist with the conviction that the way in which the patient has behaved towards him has been largely determined by interpersonal contacts, the memory of which is no longer in consciousness. At first it is difficult to understand why the patient behaves as he does, and it is not until his life history unfolds itself that it becomes clear that he is repeating earlier forms of object relationship. It was these repetitions that were identified and described by Freud as transferences.

From this point it was not difficult for some psychoanalysts to proceed to the belief that everything the patient said and did during the treatment session could be described as both repetitions and transferences. Repetition and transference were thus equated. Thus when cognition, drive and affect became less organized and infantile, as sometimes happens, it was regarded as constituting a transference from the earliest period of life. However, transference phenomena are the expression of a repetitive principle, but all repetitions are not necessarily transferences (Freeman, 1965). This view makes allowance for the fact that patients, however much mental life has been subject to dissolution, will react to the presence of another individual. It insists, however, that this reactivity, which often lacks even the most primitive type of articulation, need not necessarily be the result of a repetition of behaviours learned at the earliest nursing period. It is reasonable to assume that some of this reactivity – as in the case of perseverations and echo phenomena – is the expression of an innate repetitive tendency which leads an autonomous existence, and is only influenced secondarily by environmental experience.

Material has been presented to support the theory that the tendency to repeat is an intrinsic property of mental life. Pathological states demonstrate the extent to which environmental adaptation is deranged whenever this repetitive tendency finds an outlet in perseveration, in echo phenomena and in the living out of repressed patterns of interpersonal relationships.

Clinical evidence forms the view that this repetitive and compulsive tendency is present in the healthy, but that its expression is constantly curtailed in order that it will not disturb adaptation. The qualities of repetition and compulsion can be regarded as characteristics of unconscious mental processes, considerations which hark back to Freud's (1940) view that 'the true essence of what is mental' is not to be discovered in conscious processes. The clinical facts indicate that the concept of 'mental' includes much more than what is available to consciousness, which is only one quality of the mental and is governed by its own special laws. The remainder of mental life has another quality, an aspect of which is an innate, autonomous trend towards compulsive repetition.

CHAPTER 8

Notes on neurotic symptoms

N EUROTIC symptoms are mental and physical experiences, not due to physical disease, which are either exaggerations of normal affects with their physical manifestations, or are ego-alien. Illustrative of the former are morbid fear, low spirits without apparent cause, and heightening of the physical expression of affects without the appropriate emotional accompaniments (tachycardia, increased respiration, urgency of micturition, etc.). Examples of the latter are sensations of dizziness, loss of balance, partial or complete paralysis of a hand or arm, and compulsive thoughts and acts.

Neurotic symptoms may be the expression of the clinical entities of conversion hysteria, anxiety hysteria, anxiety states and obsessional neurosis. These are states recognized as clinical entities because of the characteristic nature of the symptomatology, the mode of onset and the course of illness. As to the nature of the symptoms, it is physical in conversion hysteria, a combination of mental and physical in anxiety hysteria, and purely mental in obsessional neurosis. The symptoms have a stability, as shown by the lack of response to environmental changes. The onset is sudden in the hysterias (conversion and anxiety hysteria), and the course of illness in anxiety states and anxiety hysteria is characterized by the development of phobias (agoraphobia and claustrophobia). Changes also take place in the personality in the direction of overdependency, and behaviour which is reminiscent of the child. However, neuroses may also occur in individuals who were always dependent on others and lacked the ability to strike out for themselves.

Neurosis and neurotic symptoms are not synonymous, for neurotic symptoms may appear in a wide variety of mental disorders. Neurotic symptoms of various kinds, phobias and obsessions may occur as prodromal manifestations of schizophrenic (pre-psychotic phase) and manic-depressive psychoses. Hysterical conversion symptoms are commonplace as reactions to psychical traumata in the battlefield. They are the presenting symptoms of adjustment reactions. In these states the precipitating factor is obvious, hence the diagnostic term in contrast to the neuroses, where immediate causes take time to identify. Lastly, neurotic symptoms also make their appearance in personality disorders of the hysterical and obsessional (reactive) type. In all these conditions the neurotic symptomatology lacks the fixity of that of the neuroses: the former are frequently ephemeral, and are sensitive to alterations in the patients' life experiences.

The self-preoccupation and the emotional egocentrism of patients who present with neurotic symptoms can be understood as a reaction to disappointments, to frustration and to the threat caused by the fulfilment or the prospective fulfilment of a wish. This reaction consists of a turning away from the unsatisfying or dangerous reality to phantasy (introversion, see Chapter 5). It is this substitution which leads to alterations in the quality of the relationships with others, for it impairs the capacity for rapport with them. However, when steps are taken, in cases of adjustment reaction, to remove the immediate causes of the illness by admission to hospital, the patient is frequently observed to become responsive to others once again. There is a corresponding diminution or disappearance of symptoms. This, as already mentioned, does not occur in the neuroses, suggesting that while the process of introversion is generally reversible in adjustment reactions it is not so in hysterical, obsessional and depressive neuroses.

The psychoanalytic explanation is that the introversion in the case of the neuroses has opened a pathway to wishes long outgrown, to memories and to phantasies of adolescence and childhood. This regression (see below) is dependent on the presence of fixations to the love objects of childhood, and to early stages of sexual development, causing psychical dangers, conflict and symptoms. The result of this regression is that the present is permanently overshadowed by the past. The fact that the symptoms of adjustment reactions lose their intensity, or disappear under the influence of changing circumstances, suggests that although there is a turning from reality, the process of introversion does not initiate a regression to fixation points.

This is not to say that regression does not take place in adjustment reactions, but it is of the type described as temporal (Freud, 1916). In contrast to libidinal regression, it is non-specific, resulting in the patient's behaviour becoming more generally childlike. This is to be observed in treatment sessions, for instance, where the patient seeks reassurance, is dependent and sometimes demanding. In neuroses, on the other hand, there is both libidinal and temporal regression.

The sequence of mental events envisaged in adjustment reactions of depression may be illustrated by the case of Nora, aged 40. Nora was admitted to hospital because of depression of mood, and a sense of hopelessness and anxiety. Her husband was a successful business man, who, some months prior to the onset of the symptoms, had had a heart attack. Until this time she had been in full, satisfying employment but had decided to stop working in order to give more time to her husband. When he recovered he decided to continue with earlier plans to expand his business. This necessitated his being out at night, and although she objected to his plans he persisted with them. If he was late home she would be seized with the fear that he had an accident in the car, or another heart attack. Then when he arrived home she would storm at him and her anger would stop her from falling asleep.

At first Nora was unwilling to speak freely about her husband. Then she admitted that she sometimes wondered if he had another woman, and was enraged at such a possibility. These ideas had been provoked because of his lack of sexual interest in her. Prior to his heart attack they had enjoyed a pleasurable sexual life together, and she could not convince herself that his loss of desire and potency could be caused by a reaction to the heart attack. When thoughts of his being unfaithful came to mind she felt sufficiently enraged to kill him. However, when it was put to her that in such a state of mind she must have had difficulty in not wishing to revenge herself by finding another man she reacted with anger. Yet when the anger subsided she admitted that such thoughts had briefly passed through her mind.

Nora's illness had been provoked by the changes in her life brought about by her husband's heart attack. In the face of sexual frustration, quite apart from the real fear that her husband might have a second attack, she turned to the phantasy of having a lover. This wish was then projected on to the husband. There was thus introversion (anxiety, conversion hysteria) to phantasy, but in contrast to a hysterical neurosis there was no libidinal regression to fixation points. The danger for this woman was created by frustration and death wishes caused by current life events, and bad conscience accounted for the depression of mood. Conscious of these thoughts about her husband her symptoms disappeared; she was not happy, but she was no longer ill.

That this woman could, with a little help, overcome the resistance opposing unwelcome wishes indicated that they belonged to the order of preconscious thoughts. This patient's symptoms, as with neurotic symptoms in general, can be evaluated from two points of view. First, they can be assessed from the standpoint of introversion and regression, and, second, from the relationship of the dangerous wishes to consciousness. In the neuroses the regression which is initiated by introversion leads to unacceptable childhood wishes which are far removed from consciousness. In adjustment reactions and reactive depression – the distinction between these two categories often being a source of diagnostic difficulty – there is introversion without regression, and the dangerous wishes are close to consciousness (preconscious).

This metapsychological approach to neurotic symptomatology also provides a means of differentiating between cases of neurosis which have identical symptoms – between those where the resolution of symptoms is easily achieved, and those where a favourable outcome requires a long period of treatment. The following cases are illustrative. Both patients suffered from attacks of dizziness, unsteadiness and palpitations which had led to agoraphobia.

The first case is that of Muriel, a married woman of 33, who suffered an acute anxiety attack in a bus. It was characterized by unsteadiness and a fear of fainting, and after two or three attacks she could not leave the house; when she began treatment the symptoms had been present for a year. It emerged that the first attack occurred soon after her husband returned from a business trip which had lasted for more than a month. Muriel and her husband had not been on good terms for some time because she believed that he had affairs with other women, although there was nothing to indicate that this was in fact so.

A month or so after starting psychoanalytic treatment she confessed that when her husband had been away she had met a man she had known in the past. He asked her out and eventually they were sexually intimate, this intimacy continuing until her husband's return. The new sexual relationship was satisfying to her in contrast to that with her husband, where she was vaginally anaesthetic. Although Nora had a bad conscience she could not stop longing for the other man and was tempted to get in touch with him despite her husband's return. She would phantasy going to see him when out shopping, and it was under such conditions that she had the first attack. These disclosures led to the gradual disappearance of the symptoms and the resolution of the phobia; the problem of the marriage relationship remained, and this became the next subject matter of the continuing analytic treatment.

Similar symptoms were experienced by Doreen, a married woman of 39 and the mother of two children. The symptoms had been present for not less than three years, but had become obscured by a depressive mood and a sense of hopelessness.

Doreen had been treated with antidepressant medications and minor tranquillizers, but none had helped her. The marriage relationship was uneventful, but she had no joy or pleasure in this.

Although the resistance exploited Doreen's difficulty in expressing her thoughts in words, a picture of the illness from its beginnings gradually emerged. The illness proper had been present since the age of 16, but an anxiety attack had occurred at the age of 14 when Doreen was visiting her grandparents. She was reading a romantic novel when she suddenly felt dizzy and had to lie down, and from this time on she was reluctant to visit her grandparents alone. When 16 years old she had the next attack, sitting in the Latin class at school: she felt a sudden dizziness and her body falling forwards. From this time on Doreen was plagued with these symptoms, and became fearful of walking alone, even of sitting in a chair. She fought against the symptoms and found methods of avoiding the situations in which she feared feeling ill; she was able to work but rarely went out socially. Her husband was her first boyfriend and Doreen came to regard him as a protector and support. The symptoms lessened progressively, and after marriage were only occasionally in evidence.

However, the symptoms recurred after a miscarriage which occurred about two years after the birth of her second child. Doreen became increasingly disabled but managed to do her housework. With reluctance she revealed that her sexual life had become unsatisfactory, because her husband suffered from a moderately severe ejaculatio praecox. This was very disappointing because she had felt herself to be responsive, and in the face of it she lost the desire for coitus and, when it occurred, had no pleasure.

Doreen had an older brother with whom she shared a bed until she was 10 years of age. She clearly recalled the sexual contact they had had, he touching her genitals and she touching his penis. This continued until she was 11, when suddenly her brother's attitude changed. He did not talk to her, becoming critical and hostile to her, and this terminated the relationship.

Subsequently she felt guilty, dreading that her mother would discover the secret.

It was a long time before the immediate cause of the illness at 16 appeared. Doreen said that at school she had fallen in love with a boy in a class above hers. At a school party she had a petting session with him and was greatly excited by this. One day while sitting alone at home, phantasying about the boy with thoughts of his marrying her, she suddenly thought of being pregnant – perhaps she was. A girlfriend had told her that kissing a boy could lead to pregnancy. She was frightened and tried to stop thinking, and the anxiety attack occurred in school the next day. One effect of the treatment was to revive Doreen's sexual wishes, thus increasing her frustration with her husband. One night, after an unsuccessful coitus which left her unsatisfied, she dreamed that she was making love with the boy at school.

In adolescence, after the arousal caused by the love-making, Doreen turned to phantasies of marriage and pregnancy. However, the process did not stop there. The available data suggested that there was a libidinal regression to fixations consti- tuted by an incestuous attachment to her brother and to phallic masturbatory excitement. The boyfriend had been chosen on the pattern of the loved brother, and a danger situation was created by the regression. Embedded within the incestuous thoughts were anxieties derived from the castration complex and penis envy. The sexual play with the brother had led to masturbation and this had been accompanied by (preconscious) wishes to re- experience the sexual games with him. Then the onset of menstruation was accompanied by the fear that she had injured herself through masturbating, and as a result she tried to hide the fact of her menstruation from her mother. It seems reasonable to assume that the miscarriage which revived the illness in its former intensity had revived the incestuous masturbatory phantasies and the fear of bodily damage: this would have been facilitated by the fact that the patient lived in a state of sexual dissatisfaction.

In contrast to the case of Muriel, the wishes which created the danger for Doreen were the result of libidinal regression and therefore, topographically speaking, were far removed from the systems conscious or preconscious. The conflict was not between the preconscious wishes of adult life and conscience, as with the first case, but were between childhood (unconscious) wishes and the remainder of the personality.

It is generally assumed that the nosographic aspects of a neurosis – for example, anxiety hysteria – are the surface manifestations of a specific psychopathological process. The symptomatology gives expression to an unconscious conflict brought about by libidinal regression, as in the case just described. However, in the first case of anxiety hysteria it was not so. From a nosographic standpoint this case was identical in all respects to the second, yet the underlying psychopathological events differed. In the former the pathogenic conflict was not the result of libidinal regression, and its topographic location was preconscious. In this respect this neurosis, like the case of adjustment reaction, had its origins in the mental consequences of contemporary events.

Such distinctions between individual cases of neurosis can only be made when it has been possible to accumulate information about each patient. Questions inevitably arise. Should cases of neurosis where the conflict is contemporary in nature (preconscious) be classified together with those others where the conflict is the result of libidinal regression (unconscious); or should they constitute a separate group analogous to Freud's (1916) category of the actual (contemporary) neurosis? These questions are not entirely academic. When they come to mind in the course of clinical work with patients suffering from neurosis they encourage enquiry which reaches beyond the sphere of symptomatology.

CHAPTER 9

A childhood orientation in adult psychiatry

M ENTAL SYMPTOMS in adults bear the hallmarks of child-hood mental life, but the identification of these signs is the more easily overlooked if there is only a passing acquaintance with the way in which healthy and disturbed children feel, think and act. Familiarity with these manifestations adds a fresh and exciting dimension to clinical practice with adult patients.

Comparisons between children and adults

Although there have been few comparative studies of child and adult patients, attention has periodically been drawn to the descriptive similarities which exist between them (Freeman, 1973a, 1976). However, recognition of these similarities has not helped to answer the question of whether or not the adult mental disorders have childhood prototypes. This has only been demonstrated in cases of anxiety hysteria (phobia states) where an almost identical symptom complex occurred in childhood, at that time taking the form of a school phobia.

School phobias occurring between the ages of 5 and 8 closely resemble the phobic manifestations which are a part of an adult neurotic symptom complex (anxiety hysteria). Then there are the hyperactive, non-organic states of childhood which are similar to the hypomanic and manic states of the adult (Anthony and Scott, 1966). For example, a boy of 5 years of age was admitted to a children's psychiatric unit because of overactivity and inability to settle in the schoolroom. He was considered to be of good intelligence, and had bowel and bladder control. According to the mother the overactivity became apparent as soon as he started to walk. This was an only child with parents who were clearly interested and concerned about his welfare: he was slightly built, inclined to be clumsy and lacking in agility. When he tried to kick a ball he usually lost his balance. In spite of his limited physical abilities, he claimed that he was 'great' at football, running and climbing. 'Did you see that great kick?' he said, when he had only managed to get his foot to the ball; on such occasions he would scream with delight and laugh. The child could not acknowledge his intellectual limitations either, and would insist on playing games which were beyond his powers. He was very distractable, and the slightest sound or movement led to his turning to the stimulus.

This little boy could be pleasant and agreeable in manner when alone with an adult. However, these periods were short-lived, being interrupted by 'grandiose' utterances such as 'What strength', after lifting a very small chair. His boastfulness had a pronounced exhibitionistic element, and he so enjoyed looking at himself in the playroom mirror that he could not concentrate on catching in a ball game. Like the adult manic patient he constantly assumed the characteristics of others. He was forever behaving like an older boy whom he clearly admired, assuming his mannerisms and repeating his utterances.

He behaved like a much younger child, where wishing transcends considerations of reality and where motility is not yet capable of being inhibited and replaced by speech. In spite of these indications of arrested development there was none of that aggressive destructiveness and sexual precocity which is a characteristic of overactive children who have suffered from emotional and physical deprivation (Rochlin, 1953; Ritvo and Solnit, 1960). Many of the utterances mentioned above might reflect the mother's concern to help him overcome his clumsiness. Furthermore, the little boy showed concern for others and for his body consistent with his experience of a loving relationship with his mother (Freud, A., 1965).

Other writers (Annell, 1971; Rie, 1966) have been impressed with childhood phenomena which appear similar to the symptoms of adult depressive states. There are also the childhood fears of contamination, dirt and disease which are reminiscent of the obsessive compulsive neuroses of the adult. Lastly, there are the similarities which exist between the wishful thinking, the egocentrism and the fears of the healthy child between the ages of 2 and 3, and the omnipotence and persecutory anxieties of the adolescent or adult schizophrenic patient.

The process of comparison can be carried further by turning to the phenomena which appear when psychotherapeutic relationships are established with adult and child patients. A woman patient who is bitterly resentful of her father's domineering manner is herself overbearing and arrogant towards the psychoanalyst. Behaviour of this kind is commonplace in children who will act the part of the angry parent or teacher. Adult patients undergoing analytic treatment describe phantasies which involve the analyst, with the patient playing the active or passive role. In these phantasies the patient is in an identification with an emotionally significant figure of his childhood and he plays the part of that person. These identifications are unconscious, in contrast to those which occur during acute psychotic attacks: there the patient assumes the physical and mental characteristics of an envied brother or sister who acts the part of persecutor (see the cases of William, Edith and Fiona, Chapters 2 and 3).

The adult neurotic patient does not know how his transference phantasies come about, although he will recognize that they are not new. He will certainly not be able to recall memories of the experiences, which comprise the raw material of the phantasies. It is left to the analyst to reconstruct the childhood events, internal and external, which provided the stimulus and the material for the phantasies. Such a reconstruction reflects the continuing presence in the adult patient of a wish to possess the attributes of the loved person of childhood, and simultaneously to participate in his or her activities. It is these wishes which lead to anxiety and to symptoms by way of substitute formation.

Reconstructions of early childhood experience frequently ring true to the adult patient. When this happens new material appears and the reconstruction contributes to an understanding of the illness. The outsider is usually less impressed, perhaps because he does not have first-hand experience of the data on which the reconstruction is based. Indeed, the criticisms of the sceptic cannot be stilled by reports of phenomena which are brought to him to scrutinize. These phenomena, which repeatedly make their appearance during the course of an analytic treatment, are only dim shadows of the vivid experience of the patient's early years and therefore it is not surprising if doubt is cast on their significance.

There is no such problem with children. It is generally accepted that young children, particularly those who suffer from morbid fears, have had experiences which are identical to those which form the basis for the reconstructions which are made in adult cases. These experiences, in the child, find an outlet through the medium of phantasy. Phantasies are expressed in play, with the child taking an active or passive role *vis-à-vis* the therapist.

A girl of 8 years of age who was undergoing psychotherapy on account of symptoms and behavioural problems had, in her last treatment session, made a passing reference to a memory of her parents waking her in the night with their shouting. When she arrived for the next session she immediately started to play a game of ghosts with the therapist. She asked the latter to pretend to be a ghost, to make 'ghost noises' and then to strangle and kill her. All this was said with great excitement. No sooner had the therapist made some mock advances when the patient suggested that they change roles. She, as the ghost, then strangled and killed the therapist, accompanying her actions with appropriate noises and shouts, but immediately telling the therapist that she was not really dead. When the therapist connected the phantasy to memories of being excited and frightened by the noise her parents made when they quarrelled, or when in bed together, the young patient immediately changed her manner. 'It's none of your business,' she said. She then picked up a toy gun and pretended to shoot the therapist. In this way she expressed her annoyance with the therapist and simultaneously repeated the impression of what she thought had taken place between her parents.

The phantasies expressed in play act as a means of representation for memories and wishes which were not available to the child's consciousness. As the clinical example illustrates, the child was afraid to remember and she acted accordingly when her memory was stirred by the therapist's interventions. Anxiety played a major part in causing the repression of her memories. However, repression does not destroy the wish to repeat what is exciting as well as frightening. As a result the repressed memories find an outlet in the phantasies, and in the way they are played out. This occurs in such a fashion, passive to active, that anxiety is abolished or reduced to a minimum.

Anxiety is also the cause of the resistance to the therapist's attempts to help the child to remember. In children the resistance follows immediately after such attempts, and it takes the most obvious forms. In the case of the adult who is undergoing analytic treatment, the resistance finds the most subtle and indirect means of expression. The analyst has to make the adult conscious of his resistance before it can be resolved. Psychotherapeutic work with children throws the phenomenon of resistance and its causes into a striking relief.

The younger the child, the less able he is to locate the sources of his wishes, sensations and emotions. They seem to have an external cause, the more so if his activities have already led to conflict with his mother. His limited vocabulary stands in the way of his being able to express thoughts, impressions and memories in words. The therapist tries to remedy this difficulty by providing the words, but whether this manoeuvre proves effective depends in part on the strength of the repression. During the analytic treatment of an adult, the therapist's interventions serve the same purpose of supplying the patient's unconscious thought processes with words so that they can become the object of his attention. Here the main obstacle is

PP-I

entirely that which springs from repression, whereas in the young child the therapist has also to contend with the rudimentary capacity for self-awareness.

The cognitive defects and the delusional experiences of a patient suffering from a schizophrenic psychosis appear less alien to the clinician who has just emerged from an encounter with a young child patient. In both child and adult wishes transcend reality. The child's tendency to repeat aloud fragments of what he has heard his parents say about himself and others, and his wishful and frightening phantasies, are to be found again in the delusional content of the schizophrenic patient. The young child's lack of familiarity with when and how words should be used (the symbolic function) leads to all kinds of mistakes in verbal expression. In schizophrenic psychoses the symbolic function is disordered: words are temporarily or permanently divorced from the objects, ideas and persons they are meant to represent – hence the double meanings, paraphasias, neologisms and faulty syntax.

A further parallel can be drawn between the young child and the adult patient suffering from a psychosis. The former's fear of an imaginary figure, representing an unacceptable wish (the wish to bite) or unacceptable part of himself (his penis), is no less intense or less real than a similar fear in an adolescent suffering from a schizophrenic psychosis. He too attributes elements of his mental and physical self to real and imaginary persons who are a source of great anxiety.

This transitivism of both child and adult dictates the manner of their initial reactions to the psychiatrist, who is seen as an extension of their mental and physical selves and therefore as a potential repository for unwanted and feared mental contents. The psychiatrist becomes a dangerous and threatening person, so a therapeutic relationship is difficult to maintain. It can in fact be achieved more easily with children, because once their fear of loss of love is relieved they can, with the help of the therapist, find a verbal outlet for the wish which was the cause of so much fear. The schizophrenic patient is not so fortunate because the morbid process, having cut him off from access to reality

(Bleuler, 1911; Freud, 1911), deprives him of this opportunity of relief.

The legacy of childhood

There has always been recognition of the fact that those who suffer from mental symptoms in adult life exhibit behaviour which is colloquially referred to as childish. This behaviour may be something new in the individual, or it may always have been a feature of his personality. This difference has been explained on the basis of there being a pathological regression affecting the personality, on the one hand, and an arrest of personality development, on the other. The latter class of patients, who complain principally of neurotic-like symptoms, are currently being referred to psychiatrists in ever-increasing numbers. When disappointed or frustrated they show extreme emotional reactions; the aggression which so frequently appears may be as easily turned against the self as against another person. They fear disapproval but under the influence of a wish of the moment they show little concern for the consequences of their actions. The occasion for the outbreak of symptoms is often the fear of loss of love, or the fear of punishment.

Like children these patients freely express their wishes and emotions once they no longer fear disapproval by the psychiatrist. When they are able to participate in a psychotherapeutic treatment, they have great expectations which are entirely based on wishing. When these are not met they angrily express their resentment and terminate the treatment. If it is continued there is a chronic sense of dissatisfaction, because their wishful phantasies cannot be fulfilled. There are always stormy reactions to the breaks in the treatment, and these are repeated when treatment is resumed. Failing to find satisfaction for their sexual and aggressive phantasies in relation to the therapist, they seek satisfactions in real life and this can be damaging to their best interests. Children in treatment show many of these characteristics and they too carry over their reactions to the therapist into the family situation.

A marked contrast is provided by patients who suffer from neuroses, depressions and the effects of a narrow and restricted personality. Instead of experiencing pleasure and enjoyment, when appropriate, they suffer from anxiety and self-reproach. The distortion of instinctual expression which leads to this state of affairs is readily appreciated by those who are familiar with the quality and content of childhood wishes, and have observed how they become transformed during the early years of life (Freud, A., 1965). Where there has been harmful interference by parents and others, these transformations come to exert a damaging rather than a beneficial effect on the growing personality.

A child of 4 years of age suffered from separation fears, intractable constipation and a compulsive need to be clean. A year or so earlier she had been referred to a child psychiatrist because of fits of crying, temper tantrums, separation fears and constipation. She was an only child whose mother had taken little part in her upbringing, and who was left each day with her grandmother while the parents went to work. During psychotherapeutic sessions, at the age of 5, she repetitively bathed a doll which she scornfully said was dirty and smelly, and she was forever putting the imaginary baby (the doll) on the potty. She was never satisfied with the 'baby's performance', and would ask anxiously if there was not more to come, and then leave the doll sitting on the pot. She would become irritable, saying in a bad-tempered voice: 'I am fed up with you' or 'You get on my nerves', which would be followed by a threat of inserting a suppository. Then she would pretend to put one into the doll's anus. It was learned later that she had struggled fiercely when given suppositories prescribed by her doctor for the constipation. During the sessions she was constantly washing her hands for fear they were dirty.

As the psychotherapy continued the girl became obstinate and negativistic. As she became less afraid of the psychotherapist, however, the negativism gave way to outright hostility when any request was made of her. Gradually her compulsive need to wash diminished, and she obtained pleasure from playing with sand

and water. As the hostile and anal-erotic wishes found an outlet her separation fears lessened and her bowel function improved. In this case, only briefly described above, it is clear that the anal-erotic and anal-sadistic tendencies had not been allowed expression at an appropriate time. Their quality, therefore, had not altered and they had become a source of anxiety because of the intolerant and demanding attitude of grandmother and mother; this was shown in the child's play. Her external conflict was dealt with by a precocious advance in ego development, which was then quite out of harmony with the fixated anality. Neither the sadistic nor erotic aspects of anality could be transformed or sublimated. Instead the anal sadism became the basis of a compulsive cleanliness and separation fears.

In adult patients such pathological transformations of instinct, which find expression in traits of personality, become conspicuous during the course of analytic treatment. No matter how hard these patients work at the analysis, they never have a sense of satisfaction. They always feel they could have done better. This dissatisfaction is also attributed to the analyst whom they are afraid they will never be able to please. They fear they will have to remain in the treatment interminably without a good result. These patients nearly always delay the expression of their thoughts as they procrastinate in everything else. When they become aware of this tendency to hold back their thoughts they want the analyst to do something to make them talk freely. These adult patients repeat what was to be observed in the young child, but they substitute words for faeces and the analytic situation for the bowel relationship with the mother, even to the extent of wishing the mother-analyst to remove the blockage of speech (faeces). They judge themselves and their performance as the mother used to do.

Healthy young children, as well as those who are disturbed, provide countless opportunities to observe how pleasurable excitement can change into anxiety and how a distaste for instinctual pleasure, whether sexual or aggressive, can establish itself. The persistence, in a female patient aged 28, of an exaggerated childhood reaction against the pleasure obtained from the pressure of a full bladder on the clitoris had led to a crushing sense of inferiority, and a fear of losing control over emotions and actions. This had its beginnings in the momentary but frequent incontinence of urine (holding on too long) which accompanied the masturbatory activity. She was severely criticized by her mother and this led to fear of the wish to masturbate. This wish was repressed, but she was left with the feeling of shame and of being inferior to others. The fear of losing control over herself resulted from a displacement from the function of urination to thoughts and action.

The normal and pathological transformations of the aims and objects of instinct which occur in early childhood (reversal of aim, changing into the opposite, displacement, regression, turning in on the self, introjection, externalization and projection) are unstable and there can be a reversion to the original form of expression under conditions of fatigue, physical illness and separation from the mother (Freud, A., 1965). It is the fluidity of the pathological transformations in childhood which allows for successful therapeutic intervention through an undoing of the distortions which have affected the instincts.

A potential for the dissolution of the transformations which the instincts undergo remains throughout life, exposing the individual to the encroachment of the original infantile wishes. The distortions of instinct which result in excessive shyness, in an over-scrupulousness in matters of hygiene and in a revulsion against masturbation are swept away during the acute psychotic attacks which occur in adolescence (see the case of Edith, Chapter 2), and replaced by a pleasure in exhibiting the body, by looking at and touching the bodies of others, by enjoying the smell and touch of faeces and by masturbation. A similar but more gradual process occurs in organic mental states.

One purpose of this chapter has been to draw attention to the need in training programmes for adult psychiatry for a much greater involvement with children than is currently the case. Diagnostic and therapeutic work with young children, and the systematic observation of healthy young children, need to become an integral part of the trainee's experience, to be continued throughout the training period. These will provide him with an additional perspective in clinical work with adults. The child in the patient will never be far from his thinking, and this will assist him in making judgements about prognosis and treatment. It will also enable him to recognize that the symptoms of mental illness are essentially exaggerations and fragmented elements of mental life which are appropriate for earlier stages of mental development.

Chapter 10

A developmental theory of psychoses

ANNA FREUD'S (1963) concept of developmental lines provides an additional perspective from which to view childhood psychopathology (Freud, A., 1965). Development along a particular line is impaired by quantitative or qualitative changes in instinctual drive endowment, by a fault in the maturation of the ego functions of motility and perception, by temporal factors which induce a too rapid or too slow development of the ego *vis-à-vis* the drives, and by the effect of errors of omission and commission on the part of the parents. These 'developmental sources of disturbance' (Freud, A., 1979) lead to disharmony and to conflict (Freud, A., 1983). Symptoms in childhood can be a consequence of these psychical disharmonies, and as such their origin lies in developmental sources.

The concept of a non-conflictual source of pathology (Freud, A., 1983) has important implications for the psychoanalytic study of the functional psychoses. The phenomena which characterize these states are not satisfactorily explained by theories based on mental conflict alone (see Klein, 1946; Blum, 1981). The fact that identical danger situations and identical conflicts are to be found in neuroses and psychoses has always led to the thought that some additional factor must be present to account for the differences in the symptomatology. Freud (1911) must have had such an idea in mind when he said: 'We can no more dismiss the possibility that disturbances of the libido may react upon the ego-cathexes than we can overlook the converse possibility – namely that a secondary or induced disturbance of the libidinal processes may result from abnormal changes in the ego. Indeed, it is probable that processes of this kind constitute the distinctive characteristic of psychoses.'

Psychotic phenomena due to loss of developmental achievements

Diseases of the brain which lead to the loss of developmental achievements frequently present with persecutory delusions, hallucinations and motility disorders no different from those which appear in the functional psychoses. There are grounds for believing that these delusions and hallucinations, which occur in organic mental states, may arise from a psychical disharmony comparable to that postulated as the primary cause of certain childhood mental disorders.

The loss of developmental achievements is most pronounced in the pre-senile dementias of Pick and Alzheimer, and in cases of senile dementia. The loss is more circumscribed but no less damaging in cases of Huntington's chorea, Korsakov's psychosis and in the early stages of cerebral arteriosclerosis. As described in Chapter 7, there will be, in varying degrees, a difficulty in recalling immediate impressions, loss of volition, an inability to initiate and terminate speech and action at will. The dissolution of the secondary process which accompanies the deterioration of the ego causes the primary process (Freud, 1900) to influence increasingly every aspect of mental life.

As described in Chapter 7, it is not uncommon, early in the illness, to encounter ideas of reference with the patient believing that he is being watched and talked about in a critical way. These phenomena indicate that psychical structures are already subject to dissolution. The superego is no longer differentiated from the ego: this loss of the superego as an internal agency is reflected in the fact that guilt feelings are uncommon in an organic mental state once the disease has firmly established itself. Evidence of instinctual regression is then forthcoming with oral and anal wishes finding satisfaction in auto-erotic activities. Violent outbursts of rage occur in individuals who were, prior to the illness, regarded as gentle and considerate. This lack of restraint is a measure of the dissolution of reaction formations and of repression.

Many of the phenomena which characterize the functional psychoses can also be attributed to the loss of developmental achievements. The acute psychotic attack occurs because of such losses and their effect persists in patients who do not reach a complete remission of the symptoms. The manic attack can be taken as a prototype illustrating the consequences of a sudden loss of developmental achievements.

In mania the superego disappears and the ego functions are entirely in the service of the sexual instincts – both genital and pregenital. Reality and the self are perceived in accordance with wish-fulfilment. The loss of the secondary process (Freud, 1900) is instrumental in leading to the condensation of object- and self-representations, percepts and memory traces. There are misperceptions motivated by wishes (primary process; Freud, 1900). The readiness to make identifications, always fleeting in nature, is matched by the externalization of aspects of the self, with resulting transitivistic phenomena. This externalization can have a defensive aim, as when a patient will accuse someone else of wishes he has already carried out. Conflict with others might follow, indicating that, as intrapsychic conflict is no longer possible, it is enacted with an external object. For the most part, real objects are only of interest in so far as they satisfy a need of the moment.

There is no less a loss of developmental achievements in acute psychotic attacks characterized by terrifying delusions and hallucinations. As with mania, there is a loss of the secondary process, but the resulting omnipotence and grandiosity is overshadowed by the dread of the persecutor(s). There is a loss of psychical differentiation which finds expression in the merging of self and object, but the ensuing appersonations and transitivistic phenomena are most often the cause of anxiety

(Freeman, 1976). It is the constantly recurring anxiety which distinguishes maniacal states from those which are variously diagnosed as schizophrenia, schizophreniform psychosis or schizo-affective state.

The content of persecutory delusions and hallucinations (functional psychoses) usually reveals the cause of the anxiety. Most often the danger is of a sexual or destructive character, but the specific details vary according to the type of the illness. Whatever the nature of the instinctual wishes may be – and their variety is considerable – they are unacceptable to the patient, as evidenced by the fact that they are a source of anxiety. Further, these unacceptable wishes are externalized and regarded by the patient as alien to his feeling and thinking. During such an acute psychotic attack there is a continuing conflict between two separate elements of the personality.

The content of the delusions and hallucinations indicates that this conflict is different from that which can be discerned in a neurosis. Apart from the fact that the site of conflict is different, the superego no longer plays the same role. At first glance it may appear as if the persecutors represent a regressed, externalized version of the superego. However, even although the replacement of consciousness of the self and self-examination by ideas of reference and by auditory hallucinations (voices commenting on thoughts and actions) can be attributed to the loss and externalization of the superego, the weight of clinical evidence favours the view that the anxiety which is experienced in psychoses springs from instinctual wishes represented by the persecutors.

The bisexual content of delusions and hallucinations expressed in a genital or pregenital (sadistic) mode, to take one example, suggests that the psychotic conflict has characteristics more appropriate to the conflicts which, in developmental terms, precede those which appear once the ego and the superego begin their final development – i.e. after the passing of the Oedipus complex. Viewed in this way, psychotic conflicts can be thought of as similar to the internal conflicts (Freud, A., 1965) of early childhood, rather than consisting of an externalization of internalized conflicts. The psychotic conflict consists of clashes between love and hate, masculinity and femininity, and between activity and passivity.

Conflict created by wishes which run counter to an already established sexual identity or caused by ambivalence can be compared with the disharmony which arises in organic mental states. Here the disharmony is not caused by conflict but by the inability of the ego, altered by organic disease and deprived of the guiding presence of the superego, to accept or repudiate instinctual wishes.

As described in Chapter 4, Katan (1974, 1979) has assembled clinical evidence to support his theory that, prior to the onset of a schizophrenia, the patient is already in the grip of unconscious homosexual wishes which will find expression in the psychotic attack. When the pressure of these wishes increases, there is conflict with the patient's established sexual identity. Defensive measures follow, designed either to strengthen the acknowledged identity or to avoid any situation which might accentuate desires for satisfaction of the homosexual wishes. Hence the appearance, in the pre-psychotic phase, of a compulsive heterosexuality in thought or action, on the one side, and avoidance measures which take the form of phobias and obsessional symptoms, on the other. The psychosis erupts at the point when the homosexual wishes, finding a transient expression, evoke anxiety of such intensity that there is a dissolution of psychical structures and an ensuing break with reality.

A developmental psychopathology of the psychoses

The theory that psychoses are set in motion by the dread of instinctual wishes is dependent on the idea that the ego organization (Freud, 1923) lacks the necessary strength to counter this threat. Yet, in cases of psychosis which begin in adult life (see Chapters 2 and 3), there is little to suggest that psychical structures (ego and superego) had not reached their full development. Once the break with reality occurs there is little similarity between the thought and feeling which characterizes the psychotic attack and that which existed prior to the attack. A contrast is provided by types of psychosis which begin in early or middle adolescence, because here connections have already been demonstrated (Freud, A., 1936, 1958) between the psychotic phenomena and mental life of adolescence.

Emotionally disturbed adolescents reveal vividly what is only to be discerned faintly in a healthy young person. There is disillusionment with the parents: they are criticized, denigrated and ignored. There may be a physical as well as a mental withdrawal from one or both parents. The new relationships which are established outside the family, whether with older persons or with contemporaries, are idealized and provide the material for what turn out to be transient identifications. There is always ambivalence, as evidenced in the ease with which hatred is evoked. The mental and bodily self is similarly the object of ambivalence. There is either overvaluation of the self, or it is despised and even hated. Omnipotent phantasies alternate with those which reflect a sense of inadequacy and inferiority. The body is both exciting and distasteful, with a revulsion against any form of bodily pleasure.

These manifestations, albeit in a grossly exaggerated form, are to be found in the psychosis which has its onset in early or middle adolescence. Complete withdrawal from the parents is often one of the first signs of the developing illness. Where withdrawal is prominent, it is always accompanied by negativism and neglect of the body. Physical movement of any kind, bodily relaxation, eating, urinating and defecating are not permitted because of the pleasure they may afford. Masturbation is a crime and sometimes the hatred for the parents can be traced to a belief that they failed to protect the patient from this evil. Excitement expressed in sexual or destructive phantasies is contained by changes in muscle tone, as in catalepsy. Once the psychosis erupts, the hatred of the parents may be expressed by a denial of their existence and the appearance of family romance delusions (see Chapters 2 and 3).

This phase of withdrawal and negativism may suddenly disappear, to be replaced by excitement and overactivity with a free expression of sexuality and aggression (see the case of Edith, Chapter 2). During such an attack the patient exhibits omnipotent delusions which mirror adolescent and pre-adolescent phantasies. Fleeting identifications also occur, along with or instead of an object relationship. This type of relating based on ('primary') identification may become a permanent feature in those cases which terminate in the hebephrenic type of chronic schizophrenia.

When the metapsychology of the first stage of symptom formation in adolescent schizophrenia or schizophreniform psychosis is compared with that postulated for the non-psychotic adolescent, it is apparent that the immediate cause of the illness lies in a miscarriage of those developmental processes which enable the young person to loosen his attachments to his parents, consolidate his sense of personal and sexual identity, and establish adult object relationships. In order to achieve these ends, there must be a withdrawal of drive cathexis from the parental objects. This withdrawal is made more urgent by the appearance of genital sexuality.

The behaviour of healthy adolescents shows that even a gradual and limited withdrawal of object libido can disturb the whole of the developing personality. The decathexis affects the object representations which comprise the ego and superego and it heightens narcissism. The outcome is a reduction in drive control, weakening of the secondary process, and impairment of judgement and the sense of reality. This regressive movement does not impair the healthy adolescent's capacity to cathect new objects, but he does so in a manner conditioned by the current state of the drives, the ego and the superego.

Adolescence is therefore a period when the ego and the superego must be sufficiently resilient to endure regression without their suffering permanent arrests and deviation. A psychosis occurs when these psychical structures are unable to sustain this tactical manoeuvre initiated to deal with the threat created by genital sexuality. To continue the military metaphor, there is a rout instead of an orderly retreat. The dissolution of the ego and the superego takes place simultaneously with the disruption of object relationships.

Theories of psychosis which emphasize the role of the strength of the instincts or the ego, and look to conflict as the mainspring of symptom formation, fail to take account of the fact that pathology, whether in the mental or physical spheres, fragments and separates. This fragmentation of healthy mental life leads to the phenomena which are attributable to the loss of the ego in its cognitive and defensive aspects, on the one hand, and to those manifestations which result from changes in the quality and distribution of the drives, on the other hand. If a theory of psychosis is to do justice to the complexity of the morbid mental events, each facet of the pathological process must be defined, their interconnections traced out, and their developmental histories discovered as far as this is possible.

The failure of the adolescent ego and superego to recover after the regression – essential if the libidinal instincts are to change direction and find new objects outside the family – and the resultant appearance of a psychosis suggests that the point of vulnerability in this type of illness must lie in the area of drive/ ego integration. In causing a fragmentation of the integration between primary and secondary processes, pathology acts in the opposite direction to the synthetic tendencies which combine the drives, ego, superego and reality into the hierarchy of organiza-tions which constitute the stages along a given developmental line. It may be said that adolescent psychoses, like any other disturbance occurring during the course of mental evolution, can be regarded as an aspect of the pathology of developmental lines.

There is another type of psychosis, occurring most frequently in late adolescence, which shows quite different features from that in which the parents figure so largely in the patient's thinking and behaviour. In this other type, relationships with the parents are secondary to delusions about a person with whom the patient had a real emotional relationship. This person or a substitute becomes a persecutor (see the case of Emma, Chapter 2). In these cases the patient appears to have succeeded in making the necessary redistribution of libidinal cathexes to free himself from the parental objects, but has found it impossible to establish a new love relationship.

It is cases of this type which give most support to the theory that it is dread of an instinctual wish which initiates the process of symptom formation. However, there are other considerations which must be taken into account. These patients are able to make a real object choice, but it cannot be brought to fruition. The object choice is made on the basis of narcissism the nature of which is qualitatively different from that encountered in healthy, neurotic and homosexual individuals. The narcissistic object represents the unconscious element of the patient's bisexuality (see the case of Emma, Chapter 2). At a certain point in the relationship the object love, founded on this narcissistic libido, is converted into hate. All these anomalies, brought to light in the psychotic attack, can only have their origins in an abnormal development.

The nature of this faulty development, which leaves the adolescent vulnerable to a psychotic attack, may be in essence no different from that postulated for those children whose symptomatology owes more to 'developmental sources of disturbance' (Freud, A., 1963) than to conflict. Such developmental disturbances and the ensuing psychical disharmonies occurring from infancy onwards might well deprive the adolescent of his psychical economy which would enable him to proceed towards adult object relationships.

The loss of object constancy (Freud, A., 1968), the intense ambivalence, the ease with which object libido is transformed into 'ego' libido and the overriding influence of the primary process during the acute psychotic attack suggest that development is adversely affected at critical periods of mental evolution. In infancy, for example, the synthesis of asynchronous elements – abnormal drive endowment and deviant mothering – lead to a weakness of object constancy.

Again, instinctual endowment and/or some 'environmental interference' (Nagera, 1966) may oppose the fusion of libidinal and aggressive instincts promoting the potential for the transformation of love to hate in object relationships. Further, constitutional or 'environmental interference' may impede the conversion of narcissistic to object libido. In early childhood the evolution of the ego can be disturbed by premature sexual stimulation, providing the source of yet further psychical disharmony. Allowance has also to be made for the bisexuality which derives from constitutional sources. These disturbances of development, which distort succeeding stages of a developmental line, will occur before psychical structures are fully differentiated, and therefore before there can be internalized conflict.

Mental conflict arising from unacceptable wishes plays a negligible part in organic mental states, in leading to the loss of developmental achievements. The fragmentation and destruction of mental structure ensures that there can no longer be the co-operation which existed in health between the primary and secondary processes. It is this asynergia, the breakdown of the integration between the two systems, which provides anxiety, delusions and hallucinations.

In adolescent psychoses there is no lack of evidence of mental conflict but, according to the view advanced here, this conflict is a secondary rather than a primary cause of the morbid process. Until the advent of puberty in the predisposed individual, the natural tendency for synthesis in mental life limits the effect of earlier disharmonies through compromise, and this allows adequate function. The new steps which must be taken in order to progress to adulthood impose an intolerable strain on these products of synthesis. Their fragmentation revives the lack of order which once existed between the drives, ego, superego and reality. In some instances it is the occurrence of a real trauma which reawakens the disharmony. As in organic mental states, the loss of integration encourages the appearance of conflict and of mental symptoms. Disharmony acts against mental evolution and promotes dissolution, with the loss of developmental achievements. It may also be that psychoses which occur for the first time in adult life result from the revival of disharmony, so promoting anxiety, guilt and symptom formation.

The psychoanalytic treatment of a borderline state

C HAPTER 11 concerns the treatment of a borderline state. This clinical concept attempts to portray patients who exhibit – amongst symptoms of anxiety, depression of mood and hypochondriacal preoccupations – an instability of reality testing. They therefore give the impression of being on the point of developing a psychotic illness with its delusional manifestations – it does not occur, however. The 'psychotic-like' features have led to the idea of a pathological mental state which is on the borderline between neurosis and psychosis.

The patient, Desmond, was a young man of 21 who was convinced that the hair of his head above his left ear was diseased. He believed that his hair, extending up onto the crown of his head, had changed with respect to both its shape and texture: while previously the hairs had been straight, they were now crinkly. Desmond was compelled to examine his hair in the mirror but the fear led him to try to avoid looking at the hair. He was convinced that others knew that his hair was abnormal, and therefore he had to remain indoors. If he touched his hair by accident, or by chance saw it reflected in a mirror or shiny surface, he became panic stricken. He could not be reassured that his hair was healthy, in spite of being told by a dermatologist that it was quite normal.

According to his story he had been quite well until eighteen months previously, when he noticed that his scalp was itchy. He consulted a trichologist, who told him that he was going bald. He became panic stricken, and found he could not eat, so avoided company.

About one year before the onset of the illness Desmond was introduced to sexual intercourse by a girl he had known at school. He was apprehensive after the act, fearing that he might contract venereal disease. Nonetheless, this relationship continued for some months. He then met a girl who belonged to a strict evangelical sect and refused to have sexual intercourse with him. She persuaded him to attend religious meetings where 'hell and damnation' was the punishment for sinners. Desmond became confused and conflicted about his sexual needs, and it was against this background that the anxiety about his hair appeared.

Childhood memories showed that, during latency, he had been overanxious and tied to his home. Starting school was difficult; he was afraid of teachers and the boys, and was shy and sensitive. He did not achieve what was well within his intellectual capacity, and felt different from the other boys. He disliked changing for games, and found it difficult to urinate when other boys were present; he thought that he must be odd when he noticed that others were not circumcised.

Desmond was most comfortable at home, sitting in the kitchen while his mother prepared a meal. He disliked the idea of giving away a toy because he thought it would be lonely. A disillusionment with the parents, particularly the father, was expressed in a family romance phantasy which began when he was about 4 or 5 years of age. At puberty he allowed himself to believe that a friend of his father's was his real father, and he told several people that this was so. He recalled that at about the age of 6 or 7 he was at the hairdresser and when he saw his cut hair lying on the floor he felt as if he had lost a part of himself.

Desmond was a keen observer and inquisitive: in latency he played at games or had phantasies in which he was a spy in enemy country. He established a hide in a tree and observed all who passed; he could not be seen or found, no matter how much he was searched for. However, in spite of his acute powers of observation and his curiosity, his knowledge of sexuality was delayed until late adolescence. By this time he had withdrawn from his father and was inwardly critical of him. He eventually acknowledged that his parents had sexual intercourse and learned how babies were born.

In the course of analytic treatment, reconstruction demonstrated pathological features of his development which threw light on the nature of the disorder with which he presented. Vicissitudes of the transference indicated the extent and quality of his emotional attachment to his parents. Periodically, until the successful completion of the treatment, there were phases of withdrawal caused by bouts of acute anxiety about the state of his hair. He was afraid that the author might die or be killed in an air or car accident. In fact these anxieties mirrored similar fears about his father, towards whom he was resentful, although this was expressed indirectly in silence and avoidance of contact. Only when his fear that the author would get fed up with him diminished was he able to reveal his jealousy of other patients, and his wish for an exclusive relationship. This again reflected a similar set of attitudes towards his mother and two younger siblings. He was devoted to his mother, yet at the same time feared and distrusted her.

A series of dreams made it clear that in early childhood Desmond had often witnessed coitus between the parents, and was also exposed to their violent quarrelling, which went on right through to his adolescence. Screen memories also confirmed the witnessing of parental intercourse. The excitement and anxiety generated by these experiences were augmented by his mother's distress on account of her psoriasis, which was principally localized to her scalp. Desmond would watch her spending hours removing the scales from these lesions; sometimes she would put some of her lotion on her son's hair. She would refuse to leave the house if she suspected that anyone might spot the blemishes beneath her hair. During the analysis the patient dreamed he had lesions indistinguishable from those of his mother.

This identification with the mother, strongly reinforced by his observations of coitus, predisposed Desmond to passive femininity, and this characterized his personality but had not entirely precluded the emergence of masculinity. He recalled a childhood phantasy in which he told his mother he would marry her when he grew up. He also related a series of dreams in which he was the active sexual partner of a woman who sometimes showed some physical characteristic of his mother. Usually he was interrupted in the middle of the love-making, or the analyst appeared in an angry mood. Following a reconstruction of these primal scenes he related the following dream: 'He is driving in a car with his mother, he reverses the car into a gateway, his father's golf clubs are sticking out of the boot and they are bent by the collision with the gate. He is upset and hits himself. Then he is with a girl trying to make love to her.'

Desmond's wish to interrupt his parents' intercourse was expressed in later memories of trying to intervene between them when they were having a violent quarrel. Through the trans-ference – the analyst was a dangerous, treacherous and frightening person – he presented some idea of how he imagined his father in early times. Furthermore, his constant complaints that he was deceived and not told the truth about the state of his hair pointed to the anger which underlay his frustrated efforts to find out what went on between his parents. Both mother and analyst were deceitful.

The death wishes which were so easily discerned, first as a transference and then aimed at the father, had never found a direct expression in conscious hatred of the father. The following phantasy is illustrative of the guilt which had resulted from the death wishes. Desmond imagined knocking a man down while driving his car and believed that he had killed him. But the man got up, unbeknown to the patient, and was killed by someone else, so the patient would never know that he was innocent. His anger was turned against himself, as in the dream quoted above, and this was also to be seen in an incident in which his father struck his mother. The patient picked up a piece of wood but struck himself on his head, cutting his scalp instead of hitting his father, which was clearly his initial intention.

After the onset of his illness Desmond dreaded the sight of his own hair, and he envied and admired the hair of other young men. Only straight hair was healthy, while his own, being 'crinkly', was abnormal and equated with women's pubic hair. He recalled a memory from childhood of watching two dogs in intercourse. The dog had straight hair whilst the bitch – a poodle – had curly hair, and he feared they were stuck together. This screen memory contained within it his phantasy of parental intercourse expressed in terms of hair – father with straight hairs (erect penis) and mother with 'crinkly' hair (castrated). In the illness he had lost his masculinity (straight hair) and feared becoming a woman (crinkly hair) like his mother.

The identification with his mother and her hair was traced back to very early childhood, prior to the conflict between masculinity and femininity which occurred with the emergence of his phallic sexuality. When he was $1\frac{1}{2}$ years old his mother had to go to hospital because she miscarried. While she was away he began to pull his hair out when asleep. This hair-pulling continued, according to the mother, until he was 3 years of age, and during that time she put mittens on his hands when he went to bed, to stop him pulling his hair out. The connection between hair and penis through touching may well have begun during that period, when he was certainly the witness of parental coitus.

All Desmond's anxieties found expression through thoughts about hair. His wish to touch his hair and his revulsion against doing so were a repetition of his conflict over masturbation. This wish to look at his hair, and the dread of what he might see, reflected his wish to see the woman's genitals. The compulsive quality of these ideas suggests that they belonged to the phallic stage of his sexual development, which had a premature arousal through the repeated witnessing of parental intercourse.

Evidence for a phallic fixation was further strengthened by the way in which he equated his body with the penis. He held himself stiffly and walked with his arms fixed to the trunk. This body= penis equation could be traced to phantasies of the latency period, when he identified himself with TV cartoon figures. The first of these was a Mr Brush, a stick man composed of an inverted garden broom with his hair consisting of twigs; the second figure was a Mr Twizzle, who had extending arms and legs.

The clinical data which have been described suggest that the following sequence of mental events led to the symptomatology. The illness was provoked initially by guilt. Genital satisfaction was no longer possible and other, past forms of pleasure were sought out. The libidinal regression affected both sexual aims and the sexual object. The self replaced the object, while looking and touching substituted for genitality. The childhood wish to look and touch his own and his mother's genitals evoked memories of the latter's pubic hair. This led to anxiety, based on castration fear, which could not be dealt with by repression.

The hair of the head replaced the mother's pubic hair and substituted for the genitalia. A connection had been formed in childhood between the hair of the head and both male and female genitalia. The traumatic repetition, with the first girlfriend, of the sight of the mother's vulva resulted in a compulsion to look and to touch that part of his hair, which was equated with his mother's pubic hair.

In common with other patients suffering from this type of borderline state, the young man was difficult to treat. These difficulties arose from a low anxiety tolerance, poor affect control, and faulty reality testing in that his perception of his hair as abnormal could not be altered by reasonable and rational argument. His judgement in this respect was no less impaired than that of the deluded psychotic patient. These features have been described as characteristic of the borderline case by numerous writers (Knight, 1953a; Rangell, 1956; Bychowski, 1956; Kernberg, 1967).

Desmond could not understand how talking could cure what he regarded as a 'physical' condition. He continued in this belief for well over a year, and it was only with difficulty that he was persuaded by his mother to carry on with the treatment. During this period he was seen face to face. At one point his agitation and sense of despair became so great that the danger of suicide became a reality; often he had to be seen on every day of the week. In retrospect, the change for the better – that is, his willingness to consider that past experiences and emotional responses might be playing a part in his illness – occurred after he came to recognize that he was behaving exactly as his mother had done in regard to her psoriasis of the scalp. The memories of her distress shocked and pained him.

As in the borderline cases which have been treated, there was a history of repeated 'environmental interferences' (Nagera, 1966) in early childhood. There were separations from the mother following on her clashes with the patient's father. There was constant sexual overstimulation, resulting from an excessive physical closeness to the mother and the repeated witnessing of parental coitus. Reference has already been made to Desmond's being witness to the mother's acute physical and mental distress. Lastly, there were the violent rows between the parents.

It is more than likely, as Kernberg (1974) and others (Greenson, 1955; Reich, 1960) have proposed, that such experiences exaggerated the patient's sense of helplessness and interfered with the healthy development of realistic identifications; hence the lack of a stable sense of self and a proper self-regard. This patient had, throughout boyhood and early adolescence, a crushing sense of inferiority, which encouraged the solitariness which characterized him. There was, however, no evidence of the compensatory phantasies of an omnipotent or omniscient kind which are believed by Reich (1960) and Kernberg (1974) to interfere with the evolution of a sound reality sense. Such overvaluation as was observable applied only to his hair. This was the expression of the pathological narcissism which had resulted from shocks and disappointments, principally in connection with the mother (object libido to narcissistic libido; object choice to identification). The direction which the withdrawing libido took was determined by the overriding identification with the mother – hence the hypercathexis of the hair and the scalp.

Despite the 'environmental interferences' which occurred during the first years of Desmond's life and led to an 'ego weakness', this young man reached the phallic-Oedipal level of development. This is evidenced by his phantasy of marrying his mother, looking after her and protecting her against his father. The death wishes against the latter and the fear of retribution found a repetition in the transference. It was a sexual encounter which led to regression and to the revival of pre-Oedipal pathology. The anxiety caused by phallic sexuality was expressed via the hair (displacement from below upwards). Regression, provoked by castration fear, affected the ego rather than the sexual instincts. New anxieties, derived from the mother relationship, heightened the castration fear. Once the pre-Oedipal pathology was resolved, a resolution of the displacement occurred with a concurrent strengthening of the ego, particularly in its function of reality testing.

There is much in the psychopathology of this case which is reminiscent of conversion hysteria. There is the fact that during the illness regression did not alter the quality of the sexual instincts (phallic); the latter were the predominant cause of conflict but subject to displacement to another part of the body, as in conversion hysteria. There is also the condition essential for the development of conversion hysteria: namely, a locus minoris resistentiae (somatic compliance, Freud, 1905). This was provided by the hair-pulling of infancy and the consequent attention given to the patient's scalp by the mother. Last was the presence of strong object ties despite the narcissistic cathexis of the self. It was this object cathexis which eventually permitted the development of working transferences.

This psychoanalytic treatment was conducted over a period of approximately three years. During that time there were two periods of hospitalization, and in which the treatment was continued. This led to the disappearance of the symptoms. When Desmond was contacted some five years after the end of the treatment there had been no recurrence of the symptoms. However, his personality remained much as it had been before the illness, still tending to be solitary and reserved. His working capacity was good, and he had passing relationships with the opposite sex.

CHAPTER 12

Treatment of the psychoses

TODAY psychoanalysts are not at the forefront in the treatment of the psychoses. This is not simply because of drug therapy: in a sense psychoanalysts have put themselves out of court. Since Bleuler's (1911) day psychoanalytic insights into the abnormal psychology of the psychoses have gradually taken hold. Thus the nucleus of the psychoses might be organic in origin, but the resulting symptoms are psychologically determined. Meyer's psychobiological approach highlighted the psychosocial influences which act on patients for good or ill.

Over and above this, psychoanalysts pioneered the group and community therapeutic techniques which are a part of current hospital practice. In the United Kingdom psychoanalysis did not have the dramatic influence on psychiatry that it had in the United States, but its effect on hospital practice was profound. The foundations of this movement were laid during the war years, when group methods of treatment based on psychoanalytic principles were introduced by Bion, Rickman and Foulkes at Northfield Military Hospital, Birmingham. Main (1946) and others extended this activity to include ward and recreational groups. The work set the scene for the therapeutic community (Jones, 1952).

Jones (1952) recognized, on the basis of psychoanalytic understanding, that the transference attachments which patients made to their immediate patient group and to the wider hospital community could be exploited for therapeutic ends. He hoped to analyse and resolve the patient's conflict not in individual therapy, but in the group, believing that through this process the patient would more easily come to identify with the values of the group and the hospital. This would help stabilize the ego and its defences, and supplement the beneficial effects resulting from insight into preconscious and unconscious conflicts.

The outcome of this work had been an acceptance of the need, in hospital practice, to foster interaction between patients, between patients and nurses, and to maximize the psychotherapeutic potential of the nurse; the beneficial effect of these measures on patient behaviour has been evident. What need, it has been asked, is there for the psychoanalyst whose work is time-consuming and limited to a handful of patients? There are also the changes which have occurred in the courses of psychotic illnesses over the past decades (Bleuler, M., 1978; Huber, 1979; Ciompi, 1980). These must surely be due to the combined effect of psychological, social and pharmacological treatments, and the influence of the latter has undoubtedly been particularly profound. It is of interest that the introduction of chlorpromazine in 1952–3 coincided with the opening of locked wards and the introduction of psychosocial measures. Psychotic patients were thus given greater freedom and social opportunities, and therapeutic atmosphere was encouraged in the hospital (Bickford, 1955; Cameron, Laing and McGhie, 1955; Martin, 1955). Did the beneficial effects of the drug therapy enable hospital staff to become more relaxed as the disturbed behaviour of patients diminished, or had a psychological change already been at work, lessening anxiety in both patient and nurse? A satisfactory answer to this question has never been forthcoming.

As far as acute psychotic attacks are concerned, whether appearing at the onset of an illness or during chronicity, the weight of evidence favours the view that drug therapy is the effective agent promoting remission, or removing delusions and hallucinations in an established case. Prior to the introduction of chemotherapy spontaneous remissions were commonplace, but where the attacks of illness were of long duration the patient was fearful and disturbed in his behaviour, and his physical as well as mental management taxed the resources of the hospital staff. When it comes to those psychoses which reach a chronic state, it is more difficult to claim that drug therapy alone is effective without the assistance of psychological and psychosocial measures.

Follow-up studies have shown that mental health is restored to the status quo ante in just less than 50 per cent of schizophrenic patients (Bleuler, M., 1978) and in a sizeable proportion of paranoid, maniacal and melancholic psychoses (Mandelbrote and Folkard 1961; Leyberg, 1965). The long-term courses have clearly been influenced by chemotherapy. This may indeed be the reason why, over the past decades, there has been, in the case of the schizophrenias, a shift from severe to mild end states and a reduction in the incidence of schizophrenias which, having commenced acutely, have been characterized by severe symptomatology continuing unabated over many years (Bleuler, M., 1978).

The fact that chemotherapy so frequently leads to the disappearance of the delusions, hallucinations and psychomotor overactivity of first attacks of illness has resulted in the speedy discharge of patients from hospital. However, readmission of these patients within the next months is extremely common. Illustrative is the case of a young woman aged 19, who was admitted to hospital in an overactive state, elated and claiming that she was due to marry her fiancé, the latter having only recently broken off the relationship. The young woman's mental state dramatically improved after the administration of moderate dosage of chlorpromazine, and she was discharged home soon afterwards. Two months later she was readmitted with similar symptoms. She had been visiting relatives in a town where she had spent a holiday with her fiancé, and the attack occurred immediately she returned home. Once again, she responded to a slightly higher dose of chlorpromazine, but on this occasion the remission did not fully develop until two months had passed. She became depressed in mood and remained so for several months, before achieving complete recovery from the illness.

Admission and discharge records of mental hospitals show that the number of readmissions of patients suffering from psychoses of all kinds far exceeds the number of first admissions of psychotic illness in any one year (Freeman, 1974, 1984b). What is the cause of these relapses? Are the patients discharged prematurely? Is the relapse the expression of the cyclical nature of the morbid process? Had the patients stopped taking their medications or were other influences at work (see Wing, 1985)?

In an attempt to answer these questions the author followed up 55 patients who had been discharged from hospital after treatment by chemotherapy alone. Positive or negative symptoms (Jackson, 1894) were found in 65 per cent of the patients. 48 patients were living with their families. 48 patients were taking their medications as prescribed on leaving hospital. Of these 48, 38 still had symptoms (65 per cent of all patients). The major factor preventing readmission was the tolerance of the families for symptoms and abnormal behaviour. Reappearance of symptoms, refusal to continue with medications, inability to participate in family life or unemployment did not necessarily lead to readmission. However, families differed in their ability to cope with patients, and two types of family could be distinguished. In one the patient was experienced as having an adverse effect on family life; in the other no such complaint was made. The readmission rate was three times higher from the low tolerance families than from those with higher tolerance for symptoms and disturbed behaviour. This suggests that the reaction of the family is another significant factor leading to readmission, over and above discontinuance of medications and premature discharge from hospital. Similar results have been published by others (Brown et al., 1962; Brown and Wing, 1974). According to these investigators half of those patients returning to what they describe as high EE (index of expressed emotion) relatives will suffer a relapse within nine months, whereas no more than 15 per cent of those returning to low EE relatives will do so (Vaughan and Leff, 1976a, 1976b).

Clinical experience, quite apart from the studies quoted,

attests to the importance of the psychological factor as a deter-minant of the course which a psychotic illness may follow. Chemotherapy has not altered this in any way, despite its beneficial influence on the delusions, hallucinations and psychomotor symptoms. If there is no resolution of the morbid process which allows the expression of these positive symptoms, the illness continues uninfluenced by chemotherapy (Wing, 1985).

Psychiatrists who acknowledge that psychical processes can be productive of positive and negative symptoms are often content to see in these processes a loss of the capacity to regulate the affects as occurs in the mentally healthy. Envy, jealousy, hatred, love, grief and sexual feeling have an anomalous expression through the symptomatology and the abnormal behaviour. Psychotherapy, group or individual, has therefore an important part to play here. Deciphering the symptomatology into the language of disturbed interpersonal relationships has its place, but the essential element of treatment must be the correction of the abnormal affective responses by drugs, psychotherapy and by social measures.

This is the therapeutic tradition of Bleuler and Meyer (Whitehorn, 1952), and the field for this approach to treatment is vast. There are the acute attacks which initiate the remitting (schizophrenoform) and non-remitting (process) schizo-phrenias, the paranoid psychoses, maniacal states and reactive psychoses. There is also the challenge presented by those patients whose illness has entered a chronic phase (Ugelstadt, 1975). It has had a considerable measure of success, as judged by numerous reports in the literature (see *Psychotherapy of Schizophrenia*, 1972, 1976, 1979). What further contribution can psychoanalysis make to the treatment of the psychoses?

The contribution of psychoanalysis

Psychoanalysts who work with patients suffering from psychoses also recognize that these are persons in whom there exists a pathological regulation of the affects. However, in their opinion this disturbance is a consequence rather than a cause. Their contribution to the treatment lies in the potential of analytic therapy to identify and recreate the nucleus of the disorder of affect regulation. This is done not only by the patient recollecting damaging experiences, important as they may be, but by the analyst taking cognizance of the compulsion to repeat. The psychotic patient, no less than the patient suffering from a symptom or character neurosis, repeats the real and imagined (phantasy) events of his early childhood. The expression of these transference repetitions is an orderly affair in a symptom neurosis, and mostly confined to the treatment situation. But this is not so in the case of the psychoses. There the effect of psychical dissolution is such as to make the expression of the transferences unpredictable with respect to the time of their occurrence, the place of their occurrence, and the person to whom they attach themselves.

From the very beginning psychoanalysts realized that the greatest difficulties stood in the way of discovering these transference repetitions, the working through of which could be therapeutic (Searles, 1963). As is well known, Bleuler, Jung, Freud and Abraham were of the opinion that transference did not occur in the schizophrenias. For Freud it was a matter of a return to auto-erotism; for Bleuler the autism was responsible. In more recent times the controversy has shifted and now revolves around what is to be included within the transference concept as it applies to the schizophrenias (Rosenfeld, 1954; Searles, 1963; Jacobson, 1967).

It has long been appreciated that it was not simply a matter of an inability or an unwillingness on the part of patients to participate in treatment. Difficulties also arose from the traditional methods of patient management and the administrative structures of the mental hospital. Many of the first psychoanalysts to treat psychotic patients understood that the detection of transference phenomena required special conditions – most importantly the education of nurses, and all those in contact with the patient, to recognize their own potential as transference objects. In 1929 Simmel established a psychoanalytic hospital in Germany where the affective accompaniments of the illness and the therapy could be accommodated. Sullivan (1932) organized special wards for the treatment of schizophrenic patients which he manned with nurses specially trained by himself. A few years later similar attempts to treat psychotic patients by psychoanalysis were under way at the Menninger Clinic, Topeka, Kansas, at Chestnut Lodge, Rockville, Maryland, and other hospitals. Modifications of the classical technique were introduced (Fromm-Reichmann, 1939, Hill, 1955; Knight, 1953b) and special attention was paid to techniques of patient management (Federn, 1953; Sechahaye, 1953). At the same time patients have been treated with minimal alterations to the technique, particularly eschewing any intervention which might be regarded as reassuring or supportive: here interpretations were confined to those dealing with the transference (see Rosenfeld, Segal, etc.). Others (Searles, Burnham) had adopted a less rigid approach, but have nevertheless concentrated their attention on the transference manifestations.

The treatment of the psychoses by a modified or unmodified psychoanalytic technique has always been confined to a handful of hospitals in Europe and the United States. This was not only because the necessary conditions in the average mental hospital were thought impracticable, but also because such institutions rarely had a trained psychoanalyst on the medical staff. Where there was it did prove possible to introduce, on a very limited scale, some of the conditions necessary for the analytic treatment of individual patients and for group analytic psychotherapy (Freeman, Cameron and McGhie, 1958).

The advent of chemotherapy for the psychoses had important consequences for psychoanalysts who worked in mental hospitals. The rapid resolution of positive symptoms by chemotherapy, in the case of newly admitted patients, led to changes in therapeutic practice and in clinical presentations following admission. As a result the psychoanalysts' contribution to these acute states appeared to be of less value than formerly. The effect of the drug therapy was to deprive the psychoanalyst of the delusional and hallucinatory contents which provide insight into the preconscious and unconscious conflicts of the pre-psychotic phase. Additionally, patients no longer disturbed and thought, by their relatives, to be cured were understandably eager to return home.

These changes led to the increase of readmissions for psychotic illnesses. What was to be done for those patients whose illness had not proceeded to a complete remission, and for those patients whose illness followed a cyclical course in spite of prophylactic drug treatment? Psychosocial measures, in the shape of community nursing services, day centres and hospitals for those patients whose family relationships are productive of relapse, frequently provide the support which encourages remission. They can sometimes help prevent further acute attacks and inhibit the emergence of the worst features (self-neglect, etc.) of chronicity. However, such favourable results are not always forthcoming.

The psychoanalyst, who assumes full clinical responsibility for in- and out-patients (i.e. acts as a general psychiatrist and not solely as a consultant psychotherapist: see Freeman, 1985b), now finds himself involved with those self-same patients. His aims are different from those who engage in psychosocial techniques: his wish is to obtain a glimpse of the patient's inner life, his psychical reality. Success leads to the discovery of the mental events which perpetuate chronicity. This is a contribution which psychoanalysis makes to the treatment of these established cases. In the following pages, then, a description is given of the problems and difficulties which are encountered when the psychoanalytic method, in its modified or unmodified forms, is employed with psychotic patients.

Manic-depressive depressions

Although it is possible to have success in treating a manic-depressive patient in the depressive phase by means of psycho-analysis (Abraham, 1911; Glover, 1955), it is often impossible to make any headway. The patient limits himself to a repetition of his symptoms, and requests or demands guidance and reassurance. This behaviour may continue indefinitely without there being any reference to current life circumstances, to family or work relationships. The only exception is when there is self-criticism for failure to carry out responsibilities as a father, mother, employee or employer. Throughout this time, which can continue for months on end, the patient is impervious to explanations or interpretations. It is only when he comes to realize that his expectation of a miraculous cure is not at hand that some reaction appears. From this time on there are frequent allusions to his dissatisfaction, but it is only with encouragement that he can admit to his disappointment and to his critical thoughts about the psychoanalyst.

This lack of responsiveness on the patient's part is usually attributed to resistance, in much the same way as would be done during the psychoanalytic treatment of a neurosis. It is easy to convince oneself or be convinced that the therapeutic impasse has been reached because of some transference phantasy which has not been brought to light. Consideration of an alternative explanation is hardly thought of because of the prevailing view that the patient's behaviour must have its origins in conflict. However, it may well be, as Katan (1979) suggests for the schizophrenias and paranoiac psychoses, that the 'resistance' of these particular manic-depressive patients does not arise from the ego, but instead results from economic changes which follow in the wake of the morbid process. In cases of manic depression which prove refractory to psychotherapy of an analytic type or to psychoanalysis, Freud's theory that all the available cathexis is confined in the 'complex of melancholia' appears to be correct. This was demonstrated in the following case.

A 50-year-old man, Arthur, fell ill with severe depression fifteen months after his wife died. He lost confidence in himself and was no longer able to work. He criticized himself inappropriately, was subject to intense anxiety, and showed a diurnal variation of mood. During the time which elapsed between the bereavement and the depression he had managed to work and lead a fairly normal life, but he had lost all pleasure in living and conducted his affairs in an automatic fashion. Arthur's first period of analytic treatment consisted of daily sessions for a period of eighteen months and then thrice a week for a further two years. After approximately one year of treatment an actively suicidal state made its appearance, and hospitalization had to be recommended. A course of electroshock therapy had a brief beneficial effect; the analytic treatment was continued and then broken off.

Arthur's wife had suffered from a severe depressive illness which continued unremittingly during the last nine years of her life. She suffered from severe agitation, and was incapable of looking after her house and family. She lay in bed, unwilling to attend to her personal hygiene, constantly seeking reassurance that she would get well; she gave her husband no peace. She was hospitalized on many occasions and treated with electroshock therapy, without any lasting good effect. Several attempts were made to treat her psychotherapeutically, but all came to nothing. Arthur remained well throughout all this time, in spite of the great stress to which he was subjected daily. The immediate cause of his breakdown was the departure of his only child, a daughter, to a university in a distant part of the UK. About this time, that is, about thirteen months after his wife's death, he became friendly with a woman and was soon dependent on her.

As with so many patients of this kind, Arthur's thoughts were confined to his suffering. His dead wife did not come to mind except in associations to dreams, which were few. The harrowing experiences of the nine years during which his wife was mentally ill had no place in his consciousness, and it was again through the occasional dream that some memory of these times briefly returned. Then, too, throughout the whole period of the treatment he showed no sign of interest in the author. He tried to conceal his disappointment with the latter's efforts to help him, and he tended to avoid expressing wishes for another form of treatment which he had heard or read about. There was no evidence of a working transference and interpretations which were made on the supposition that transferences existed had, understandably, no effect.

Arthur's lack of interest, on the one hand, and his wish to be made better, on the other, paralleled his attitude towards others. He was at ease with his woman friend, where his dependency wishes were gratified. He feared that she would leave him, and he also feared that the author would abandon him. However, discussion of this fear did not lead to new material nor did it ease his anxiety. If he had a pleasant outing with his woman friend his depressive symptoms were even more pronounced the next morning. This patient illustrated Freud's (1917) comment that in depressions which follow loss, even a new love object cannot wholly attract to itself the cathexis which remains invested in the lost love object.

The resistance which prevented this patient recalling memories of his dead wife was due to an unwillingness to remember the hatred and death wishes which he had borne against her. Her illness had destroyed both his opportunity for happiness and, perhaps more importantly, opportunities for advancement in his career. As has been mentioned, dreams were few, but all led back to his wife. Occasionally some element of the manifest content led to the recovery of a memory of a situation in which he had felt a keen anger against his wife. However, no affect ever accompanied these memories, showing that the repression was still operative. As in other cases of this type, the conflict of ambivalence was unconscious during the illness, but its being made manifest did not allow the libidinal cathexis to be detached from the representation of the lost love object.

The self-criticisms which this man expressed were, in fact, memories of criticisms he had made of his wife when she was alive. One of them was that he was a malingerer; others must think this too, because in the evenings he was able to feel and behave almost normally. When his wife had shown this fluctuation in her mental state, he criticized her on the grounds that she was not really ill, only pretending to be unwell for his benefit. This form of self-reproach was only one of the many which could be traced back to criticisms he had made of his dead wife.

Lack of improvement after the $3\frac{1}{2}$ years of analytic treatment led to its termination by mutual agreement. During the following two years there were severe exacerbations of the illness, and this led to periods of hospitalization. There treatment by drugs and electroshock therapy was ineffective. During this time Arthur remarried the woman he met after his first wife's death. However, his new wife's interest, support and affection did not materially influence his state. At the end of the two years he contacted the author and asked to recommence treatment with him.

A few weeks after starting it was apparent that a change had taken place in him: he appeared to be less passive in his approach to the treatment and was willing to take some responsibility for its progress. He was responsive to the idea of gradually giving up the antidepressant medications, and began to speak about his life; the former preoccupation with his symptoms lessened. Now he talked about his wife and his concern as to how he might rehabilitate himself. Memories of his childhood and adolescence came to mind. He said that from an early age he had withdrawn from his mother, who, he felt, was more interested in his younger sister. He had been very fond of his father and had a good relationship with him. (This fact had never emerged during the previous period of treatment.) The father had died when Arthur was an adolescent, and this had a profound effect on him; it was the first of a series of disappointments which culminated in his wife's illness. Arthur came to recognize that each disappointment had the significance of a betrayal: the first analytic experience was a repetition of this and, as in the past, the resulting hatred had been repressed. Over the next year he continued to improve. He began to enjoy life again and found a new occupation which was satisfying to him. Followed up two years after termination of treatment, which lasted about two years, Arthur was found to be well and free of symptoms.

Why did this man's illness fail to respond to treatment? He had lost interest in life and had turned in on himself; he had changed physically as well as mentally; he had become like his wife in physical appearance. He had become as uncertain, anxious and lacking in self-confidence as she had been. His self-reproaches were repetitions of the criticisms he had made of her. Phenomena such as these are the basis of the explanation of why seriously depressed patients are refractory to analytic treatment (Freud, 1917; Glover, 1955). The phenomena reflect the complete identification with the lost object. However, the opportunity to treat this patient for a second time, when he was able to join in a therapeutic alliance – a purely spontaneous development and independent of any specific measure on the author's part – provided a possible reason for the failure to recover. There is much to favour the view that throughout the five years or more of the illness Arthur compulsively repeated the role of a disappointed and betrayed man. The lack of object cathexis precluded the possibility of this repetition becoming available as a transference which could be used for therapeutic ends. Was this compulsive repetition due to guilt or to hatred which could only find expression in being the one who, through the illness, disappointed and betrayed? There were also other external factors, which cannot be gone into here, which may have contributed to the change which took place in this patient.

The repression which operated in this and other cases of depression is qualitatively different from that which is encountered in neuroses. There it is amenable to resolution through interpretation and working through. Failure to bring about this resolution in depressive states, as mentioned, is related to the fact of the patient's complete identification with the lost love object. While the identification continues it acts as a form of repression, depriving the hate of its real object. Only when the object cathexis is restored, following the dissolution of the identification, will the hatred no longer be subject to 'repression'.

The conflict between love and hate which is represented in the symptomatology is only one aspect of the psychical change which leads to the illness. Only when there is a change in mental economics can the conflict become sensitive to the methods which are effective in the neuroses. Until then the 'complex of melancholia' (Freud, 1917) remains active, 'drawing to itself cathectic energies – which in the transference neuroses we have called anticathexis – from all directions and emptying the ego until it is totally impoverished' (Freud, 1917). It is this impoverishment which leads to the loss of will, to the psychomotor retardation and to its subjective accompaniments.

Remitting and non-remitting schizophrenias

All psychoanalysts agree that patients suffering from schizophrenic psychoses are capable of relating to others. Controversy arises over the question of the quality of those relationships, their significance, and how far they can be employed for therapeutic ends. There are those who subscribe to the concept of a transference psychosis (Rosenfeld, 1954; Searles, 1963). This is a useful clinical concept because it describes a series of phenomena which characterize the way in which the patient relates to the psychiatrist, or psychoanalyst. There are the transitivistic signs, the appersonations, negativism, the confused speech and the persecutory ideas. However, these 'transference psychotic' phenomena are not specific to the therapeutic situation. They are to be observed with nurses, other patients, occupational therapists and other doctors. They are similar to what Glover (1955) called 'floating transferences' and are to be distinguished from the repetitions of childhood object relationships.

During the acute attacks which occur at the onset of remitting or non-remitting cases of schizophrenia, the transitivistic signs, the appersonations and persecutory ideas preclude meaningful verbal communication between patient and psychoanalyst. It is doubtful if the patient reacts to anything other than the affective tone of the analyst's interventions. During acute phases of the illness the patient does not discriminate the clinician from himself, nor the objects of his past from his own mental image or that of the clinician. Once the illness has established itself (non-remitting cases), withdrawal and negativism can add to the difficulties presented by these manifestations, and block a therapeutic relationship. However, there are also cases of non-remitting schizophrenia where some affect expression remains. The patient is friendly in manner and not averse to talking about his experiences.

Initial impressions in cases of this kind are generally misleading. After some weeks or months of regular treatment sessions, during which the patient brings forward memories and current experiences, silences develop and a loss of interest becomes apparent. Sometimes the clinician is drawn into the patient's delusional reality, either being regarded as an agent of the persecutors, or as being affected by the persecutors as the patient believes himself to be. Observations made during the attempt to treat Fiona, described in Chapter 3, will illustrate some of these points.

Fiona was pleased to have someone listen to all that had happened to her. This was her third period of hospitalization, the illness having been present for over five years. The voices she heard were a mystery to her, and she tried to explain how they arose. When the voice spoke, it could be a man or a woman, she could feel her facial muscles contract, her mouth and tongue move. Someone took possession of her powers of speech. Others were also affected in a similar way (transitivism).

After about four weeks of daily meetings she became increasingly silent. What was the cause? The author decided to act as if he were confronted by a resistance of the kind encountered during the treatment of a hysterical neurosis. He said that she was fearful of finding herself having thoughts about him; her first response was 'No'. After a minute or so she reported that she had heard the voice say 'I like his shoes.' She fell silent again. When the interpretation was repeated she said that she had noticed that the author had passed his hand over his eyes. She took this to mean that she should lie down on the couch in the room. These were her own thoughts. She then said that she had gone for a walk with a male patient the night previously, and he had tried to have intercourse with her. She heard a man's voice say, at the time, 'You're not going to do that.' Later the voice said, 'You're not too old to be hit.'

In the next sessions Fiona's communications were of a sexual nature, and her meeting the male patient on several occasions was the most likely cause of this. She reported that a voice had said: 'Do you remember that?' and automatically her lips had come together in a kiss. 'How's about a kiss?' the voice said, and her mouth moved in a kiss-like manner. At this time and on several previous occasions the author had told her that the voices she heard were her way of recalling memories of things said to her, and they were at other times a vehicle for thoughts she did not want to know about.

She appeared to understand, and in this session went on to recall a sense of sexual excitement when a boy kissed her and when a schoolmaster had put his arm round her waist when she was 15. She followed this by an account of her masturbation, which began about the age of 5. Fiona would press her genital area against anything hard. Later she would excite herself when climbing a rope in the school gymnasium; in adolescence she would try to insert the end of a clothes brush into her vagina. She always felt very guilty; she had also feared she might be a homosexual because in middle adolescence she and a girlfriend had acted heterosexual coitus, with herself as the man. While recalling these memories she experienced what she called a fuzzy feeling in her genitals. She said someone was making this happen. She added: 'I think the police are outside, the fuzz you know.'

In subsequent meetings there was a change. Fiona attended, but seemed less interested and concerned lest her wish for the session to be ended might offend the author. 'You'll be getting fed up with me, wasting your time,' she said, explaining her silence as being due to the fact that she did not have words for thoughts. She adamantly refused to consider that she was afraid of thinking about the author. She said she was more frightened by the idea that the voices came out of her own mind.

She did reveal that she heard the voice frequently during the sessions but did not want to report what was said. With encouragement she said that the voice had announced in an aggressive way: 'Do you want to know something?' Or her hallucinations consisted of 'Don't tell him any more', 'He's watching you.' The ideas expressed in the hallucinations were quite alien to her. She wished she could tell the author more; she did not regard his interest as an intrusion. At this time the nursing staff reported that she had become very withdrawn and solitary, and she was constantly asking to go home. Throughout her stay in hospital she was receiving moderate doses of an antipsychotic drug. From time to time she did not attend for the sessions and had to be sought out. Then she would sit silently and after some minutes ask to leave. It was decided to terminate the meetings, as the contact appeared to be doing more harm than good.

With non-remitting cases of this type it is possible, as Freud (1916, p. 423) put it 'to cast an inquisitive glance over the top of the wall and spy out what is going on on the other side of it'. The single most important observation to be made in these female patients is of an inordinate fear of sexual excitement. This is the cause of the 'resistance', and it cannot be dissipated by the interpretative technique normally employed in hysterical neuroses. Why are these patients so frightened? Does the fear arise from the content of the excitement? In this case, as in others, the first delusion to appear was incestuous in kind. Fiona believed her brother had raped her while she was asleep. She attributed her excitement to him and was terrified of him. As has been mentioned in Chapter 5 many psychoanalysts do not find the incestuous element sufficient reason for the anxiety. They prefer to believe that this is caused by destructive pregenital phantasies connected with the mother. What can be agreed upon, however, is the fragile nature of psychical structures. These disintegrate when faced with the anxiety caused by sexual phantasies, psychically fulfilled, whatever may comprise their nucleus.

As far as the remitting types of schizophrenia (schizophreniform) are concerned, the psychoanalyst in the mental hospital is most likely to be asked to treat those patients whose illness follows a relapsing or cyclical course. Usually the content of each acute attack is a replica of the one before, although there are exceptions to this. These cases offer the analyst a particular opportunity to treat, over an extended period of time, those instances where depressive symptoms have not responded to chemotherapy. The patient is often eager for help, and is responsive to the idea of treatment which may last over a period of time. Not infrequently symptomatic improvement is interrupted by an acute attack with persecutory delusions. The immediate causes of the relapse may be witnessed at first hand (Freeman, 1976). It is also possible to observe the transformation of the psychical dangers engendered by life events into the content of the delusions (see Chapter 4). As the acute attack subsides, this knowledge can be used in the treatment process.

In those cases where the resolution of the first acute attack is not followed by depressive symptoms or hypochondriacal preoccupations, patients are usually reluctant to enter into an ongoing psychotherapeutic relationship. In this respect they are similar to patients whose illness is of the non-remitting variety. The 'resistance' usually takes the form described above in the case of the female patient; illustrative is the case of Peter, described in Chapter 2. This was his first and, as it has turned out so far, his only psychotic attack. He was seen daily for several months, and in the same way as the (female) case of non-remitting schizophrenia.

He, too, talked freely and appeared to value the opportunity to speak about his thoughts and feelings. Not surprisingly, in view of an element of his delusional complex (the evil professor), he repeatedly referred to how he felt and reacted to older men, in particular the curator of the museum and his father. His mother, however, was the chief object of his criticism. He blamed her for his lack of self-confidence and his timidity. At school he liked the male teacher who taught him geography; it was he who advised him on the course which he was now following at university. During his last years at school he was convinced that this teacher was 'synchronized' with him: he always knew what this man thought, and he knew whatever questions he was going to be asked. He had concluded that the reason for his closeness with the teacher lay in the fact that his mother had told him that he (the teacher) had been in love with her sister.

After a period in which he had appeared to enjoy expressing

his thoughts and recalling the past, Peter found himself with nothing to say in the treatment sessions. He was forever asking how long he would have to remain in hospital. By this time the delusional ideas had receded and he appeared to have returned to his pre-illness state. Did his repeated references to his father, to the curator of the museum, and to his teacher indicate that his 'resistance' to continuing the treatment was due to anxiety springing from transference phantasies? The considerable clinical improvement led to his parents agreeing to his wish to be discharged from hospital. After leaving and ceasing attendance as an out-patient, he remained well and resumed his studies. More than four years later there was no sign of a recurrence of the illness.

In this case the acute attack was preceded by a phase, during the patient's first university term, when he was sexually aroused by a girl and he wanted to act on this. The love object had a homosexual association, in that the girl appeared to possess the physical characteristics of a male lecturer. He turned to a group which called itself the Sexual Reform Society to help strengthen his heterosexuality, for the arousal of his sexuality had made him anxious. He said he feared the girl was 'too fast for him'. A regression of the libido to homosexual phantasies may be suspected, and heterosexual object choice was abandoned in favour of identification. This type of identification, which sometimes leads to overt homosexuality, may have contributed to the heightening of unconscious feminine wishes – the wishes which had until now remained in repression.

It may be suggested that the phantasy of acting the woman with the curator led to anxiety and to psychical dissolution. A psychotic identification replaced object cathexis (see Chapter 4). This identification acted in the service of wish-fulfilment and of defence. Peter was now the admired homosexual love object (the curator), and as such omniscient and heterosexual. This patient differed from others, patients who claim that they are persecuted by a formerly loved or admired person of the same sex, in that a phantasy persecutor made an appearance (the evil professor he had to expose). This substitute for the curator and father enabled him to preserve his relationship with the latter, which suggests that cathexis was not wholly withdrawn from object-representations.

Once this threat was removed the libidinal cathexis could return to invest phantasy heterosexual objects and have its outlet in masturbation. There was no need, therefore, for a continuing defence against the passive-feminine wishes, nor were homosexual objects any longer a cause of anxiety. The fellow student who spread the rumour represented that part of the patient's self (his masculinity) which was in conflict with his feminine wishes.

What is the cause of the 'resistance' which so frequently disrupts treatment? Is it entirely due to a terror of instinctual derivatives whatever their content? There is another factor, not always given sufficient emphasis – namely, that dread of reliving the experiences of the acute psychotic attack. There is much to commend the view that a patient's ability to persevere with a therapeutic relationship depends on his capacity to overcome the memories of such attacks. This fear is enhanced by the very means by which it is hoped to cure the illness, for the analytic method encourages psychical regression. In non-psychotic patients it is this regression which allows the repetition of pathogenic conflicts as transferences, whereas in the psychoses the regression accentuates the destabilization of psychic structures. As the patient emerges from the acute attack there is a constant dread of the consequences of this destabilization – a dread of the return of the mental state caused by confusion which existed between phantasy and reality, and between self- and object-representations. This indeed may be the principal cause of the 'resistance' which so many schizophrenic patients manifest.

Assessment of the therapeutic task

Clinical experience has demonstrated that it is misleading to rely on the presenting symptomatology of psychoses as a basis for judgements regarding course of illness and response to treatment. Identical symptoms may have different structures, as in the case of anorexic symptoms in adolescent females, or homosexual anxieties in young men. It is necessary to have a means of evaluating the presenting clinical phenomena, in order to arrive at some tentative conclusions about the psychopathology.

When it is impossible, for practical reasons, to provide psychotherapeutic assistance, the knowledge gained from a detailed metapsychological study will alert the clinician to the dangers which a patient will have to face whenever he or she leaves hospital. A woman suffering from a paranoiac psychosis provoked by death wishes against her husband will still have to contend with these wishes whenever she leaves hospital. It will be no surprise if, in spite of drug therapy, there is the reappearance of her delusion that she is being watched by the police, and that her house is being searched, when she returns home. The same will be true for the woman whose persecutory delusions spring from a repressed homosexuality.

A metapsychological assessment can be made with the assistance of profile schemata (see Appendix). This enhances clinical observation and description. Phenomena which might escape notice or not be given their proper importance are brought to the forefront of the clinician's deliberations, and an interplay takes place between observation and conceptualization. Profiles illustrate how far and in what way a patient is divided against himself. Clinical experience indicates that the manner in which these conflicts are dealt with is decisive for the nature of the symptomatology and for the course of the illness. Whether the conflicts are transient or permanent, externalized or remain within the self depends on the conditions governing the functions of the drives, the ego and the superego.

As the clinical illustrations presented throughout this book have shown, the potential for internalized conflict is absent or deficient when psychical structures have failed to develop, or where these structures have been damaged by dissolution. The construction of profiles is a valuable preliminary work which can lead to fruitful discussion of programmes of treatment for individual patients. While it is impossible to generalize from the particular to the general, because of the number of intermediate types of an illness, profiles offer a means of establishing criteria to assess prognosis and treatment.

The fact that the majority of those who treat psychoses have found it necessary to modify the analytic method – which gives priority to the analysis of transference and resistance – itself points to the fact that the intrapsychic conditions existing in these disorders are different from those obtaining in the neuroses. Changes have been introduced in the formal aspects of the treatment – relaxation of the rule of free association, greater flexibility in such matters as length and frequency of sessions, and the assumption of the recumbent position. Emphasis is principally laid by some psychoanalysts on the wishes and fears which lead to the misinterpretation of reality (see Fromm-Reichmann, 1939; Federn, 1953), while other analysts also make use of their reactions to the patient to illustrate the latter's use of projective identification (see Rosenfeld, 1954; Segal, 1951).

What has been said is, in part, based on the work of many psychoanalysts with patients suffering from psychoses. Different methods (Sullivan, 1932; Fromm-Reichmann, 1939; Rosenfeld, 1954; Searles, 1963) have had their quota of successes and failures. It is because of these outcomes that doubt must be cast on the specificity of technical recommendations, and on the theories on which they are based.

It is unlikely, therefore, that the omission of a particular interpretation in a case of psychosis will endanger the treatment. As already mentioned, symptomatic relief can result from a wide variety of psychological treatments (individual, group, family therapy) as well as from chemotherapy. Spontaneous remissions also occur in cases where there are contraindications to physical forms of treatment. Sometimes these spontaneous remissions follow changes in life circumstances, as in patients who, after suffering from severe depressions which have continued over years, recover after the death of a close relative. All that can be maintained with certainty is that the therapeutic task in cases of psychosis is always onerous, and the outcome uncertain.

The psychoanalytic examination of a psychotic state

THE PROFILE schema which was constructed for the psychotic patient (Freeman, 1973b), based on that developed for the neurotic adult (Freud, A. et al., 1965), was predominantly concerned with presenting a metapsychological assessment of the presenting symptomatology. The disturbances caused to the drives, to the ego and superego by the morbid process were taken up in turn and evaluated in dynamic, economic, topographic and structural terms. This provided information about the conflicts which were present, the danger situations which had to be faced, the defences which had been called into play, the alterations in mental economics which gave the psychosis some of its characteristic features (overvaluation of the persecutors, etc.), and also pointed to the influences which these dynamic and economic conditions exerted on the function of the ego organization. Less attention was paid to the psychical conditions which had immediately preceded the onset of the psychotic attack, that is to the pre-psychotic phase. This omission has the effect of creating an artificial division between the patient's mental life as it was during the attack and as it was before the occurrence of the first signs of the illness (pre-psychotic phase).

In the vast majority of cases information about the pre-psychotic phase can only be obtained, after the onset of the psychosis, from the patient himself or from his relatives. This sort of information, in conjunction with the phenomena of the

acute attack (Katan, 1979), provides the basis for a reconstruction which, when completed, throws light on the danger
situations and conflicts which, it is presumed, led to the
symptoms and to the abnormal behaviour which preceded the
acute attack. For example, the accusations which women who
fall ill with a hypomania or a paranoid psychosis make against
their husbands do not reach consciousness during the pre-
psychotic phase. Then they only find an outlet in a depressive
mood or in self-criticism. These symptoms reflect the conflict
which has been generated by death wishes. As has been illustrated in the case of schizophrenic psychoses, the means
whereby aggressive and sexual wishes are altered by the
psychotic process are themselves a sign of the conflict which
ensued before the psychotic attack began (Freeman, 1973b).

In order to reconstruct the pre-psychotic phase it is essential to
obtain as much information as possible about the patient's
psychotic experiences. These must then be treated in the same
manner as the manifest content of a dream. The pre-psychotic
ideas can be regarded as analogous to the latent dream thoughts
which have been transformed by the dream work. In the case of
the psychotic patient the task is to identify the processes which
undertake the transformation of wishes, phantasies and
memories. As in the dream, individuals of emotional significance may not appear in the delusional content, or only find
expression through substitutes. Equally, aspects of the mental
and physical self may be represented by one or more of the
persecutors. The criticisms voiced by unknown individuals
(auditory hallucinations) are not only to be thought of as an
expression of the superego, but also as memories of parental
criticism brought up to date with the help of a contemporary
theme. As in a dream, due allowance must be made for the
effects and influence of what remains of the normal personality.

The comparison between the manifest dream and the
psychotic symptoms can be carried further by recalling that in
both dream and delusion the ego organization has lost much of
its power as a consequence of the state of sleep in the case of the
dreamer, and as a result of the dissolution of the personality in

the case of the psychotic patient (Katan, 1960). In both, the ego contribution is much less than in the case of hysterical symptoms, which are the outcome of a compromise. The transformation which affects the wishes and phantasies of the pre-psychotic phase is, as in dream formation, carried out by mechanisms which are integral elements of unconscious mental life: namely, displacement, condensation and symbolism. As in the dream (Freud, 1900) displacement plays the major part in these transformations. They owe little or nothing to the ego (Katan, 1979), nor can they, when that organization has already been disordered by the psychotic process.

When a reconstruction of the pre-psychotic phase is successful it reveals the nature of the conflict which preceded the onset of the acute attack, and which had played a decisive part in the patient's personality development. This conflict acts as a signpost to those parts of the personality which failed to achieve an optimal development. The case of an unmarried man of 27 years of age can be taken as an example. He was admitted to a mental hospital with frightening delusional ideas. He said that the Roman Catholic Church, in which he had been brought up, was determined to kill him. He had let the church down. In the street, people looked at him and he had heard references to himself on the radio and on the television. He believed that he was being accused of being a murderer. He had been treated by psychiatrists in the past and they too had wanted to kill him. At times he thought he heard voices criticizing him as a masturbator. He could not go to the police because they discriminated and attacked men whom they thought had been 'mollycoddled' and overprotected by their mothers.

This was not the patient's first attack. He first fell ill when he was 20 years of age, at a time when his mother was mentally ill. She committed suicide a year later. He suffered an acute psychotic attack in which he claimed that he was Christ. At church he had noted his face and arms altering with changes that he perceived in the face and arms of a statue of Christ. Like Christ, he was tempted. He said that to purify himself by repeatedly washing, he used a whole bar of soap for his hands alone, then his arms, legs, feet, etc. He scrubbed his nails to the quick and caused a severe irritation to the glans penis with the scrubbing brush. He claimed that while in the bath God had had sexual intercourse with him (per anum).

A second attack occurred three years later when he was 24 years old. In the intervening period he had kept quite well, following his trade and having a sexual (coital) relationship with a girl. However, he was never free of guilt over his sexual activity nor did he ever feel at ease in the company of men. He was convinced that they despised him. He gave up many jobs because he could not face his workmates. The third attack followed his being abandoned by his girlfriend. She could no longer tolerate his moral scruples. On this occasion he complained of people staring at him, laughing at him because he was a masturbator and not a proper man. He feared he was possessed by the devil.

The patient's statement showed that, in the absence of a heterosexual partner, he was constantly oppressed by the need to masturbate. After the act he felt guilty and was left with a sense of disgust. During the first psychotic attack he had washed compulsively to rid himself of (sexual) filth. This washing prevented masturbation by injuring the penis. The need to give up masturbation became increasingly urgent during the pre-psychotic period that preceded the last psychotic attack. He turned to the church for help (see below). The delusional idea that he was a murderer suggests that he believed the mastur-bation made him a murderer. It was because of this dread that he had sought help through prayer and confession. His belief that he had let the church down was the result of the reversal of his anger against the church, for not protecting him against the wish to masturbate.

The patient's state of mind during the pre-psychotic phase which preceded each attack can be attributed to the predominant anal-sadistic orientation of the libido which established itself. Genital wishes (pre-illness) have been transformed into sadistic wishes, with coitus now having the significance of murder.

Active and passive genital wishes which had a previous outlet in masturbation were now replaced by sado-masochistic phantasies. His hatred of self, expressed in self-reproaches and in suicidal attempts during the pre-psychotic phases, resulted from the reinforcement of the superego by sadism. The pre-psychotic phases lasted for as long as the anal sadism could be held in check. Avoidance of masturbation had a priority in this respect, acting as it did as a channel for the expression of the active and passive aims of the anal-sadistic libido: unconsciously he murdered and he feared being murdered. Masturbation made one or other a reality.

This man's pre-psychotic conflict provides the key to an understanding of his pre-illness personality. He apparently achieved genitality and heterosexual object choice, but his sexual life was fundamentally influenced by anal sadism. The same was true of his personality. His sense of unworthiness, the shame and disgust over his sexual needs, the lack of initiative (passivity), the intense ambivalence which characterized all relationships, and the shyness with women and oversensitivity with men must be regarded as derived from anal sadism.

The second part of a psychoanalytic examination of a psychotic illness must take up the issue of the patient's early childhood, in the hope that whatever can be reconstructed will reveal something of the psychical conditions which prevailed in these years. The symptoms of the acute attack can be used for this purpose and in the case just quoted can continue to be used as an illustration.

In the acute attacks both active and passive sexual wishes, continuing in anal-sadistic form, found expression in consciousness. This was denied to him in the pre-psychotic phases. For a brief period during the psychotic attack the anal-erotic component of the libido found an outlet in the delusion that God had coitus with him per anum. However, in subsequent attacks both masculine and feminine sexual aims were represented in the fear of being a murderer and in the fear of being murdered.

Neither mother nor father were represented in the content of the delusions and the hallucinations, but he talked at length about his father, who, he felt, had let him down by not encouraging his masculinity. If his father had paid attention to him he would have become a proper man. As it was he grew up under the influence of his mother, was tied to her 'apron strings' and as a result became timid, fearful and lacking in self-confidence. At the same time he described his father as lacking authority in the family and deferring to his wife.

While in hospital it was obvious that his self-esteem depended on how older men regarded him. If they were supporting he felt good, but if they seemed indifferent to him he became low-spirited and self-critical – 'They think I am a cissy.' These doubts and fears about himself would reach a peak of intensity whenever he masturbated, when he would imagine that he was being criticized and ridiculed by older men. He avoided the company of women, particularly older women, for fear they might try to mother him and make him feel a weakling, 'a mother's boy'. He was always ill at ease with young women. Even those with whom he had been sexually intimate in the past had never accepted him as a man.

He had little to say about his mother. This can be contrasted with his constant criticism of his father. However, his attitude to older women and his delusional ideas about the church are evidence of the intense ambivalence which must have characterized his childhood relationship with his mother. He felt a vicious anger against the church – 'They destroyed my youth, preventing me from masturbating and stopped me becoming a man.' In the psychotic attack the church acted as a substitute for his mother. His fear that the church wanted to kill him followed from a projection of his death wishes against his mother. It is hardly surprising that his first psychotic attack occurred some months after she tried to kill herself.

This man's protest against the passivity imposed by his mother must be seen against the background of the delusion that God had coitus with him per anum. In childhood he found pleasure in his mother's interest in his body and in his anal region in particular. This included the insertion of suppositories into his anal canal for constipation. At the same time, out of anxiety, she had stifled his adventurousness and his wish to be physically active. She had banned the genital excitement (masturbation) which her excessive attentions to his body had provoked.

The hypothesis that this man's hatred of his mother was the result of an unconscious envy of the pleasure she obtained from coitus with his father as well as a reaction to his masculinity, is supported by the observations which can be made during the psychoanalytic treatment of cases of anxiety hysteria in men. Where there is hatred of the mother of this intensity, behind it lies concealed the unconscious wish to be a woman, along with a 'masculine protest' which is lived through in the transference as well as in the current heterosexual relationship.

Everything points to the conclusion that a fixation of the libido was established at the anal phase. The fixation acted against the emergence of a sound Oedipal development. This may have been momentarily achieved, and evidence for this assertion will be given below. However, regression soon led to a reawakening of the anal erotism and to the passive attitude to the father. At puberty some development towards genitality took place, thus overlaying the anal-sadistic tendencies. Nevertheless, they had their effects on his personality make-up which was characterized by reaction formations against dirt and cruelty. During the psychotic attack he protested against the cruelty which the police were inflicting on men they thought of as being 'mother's boys'.

The advent of puberty saw the appearance of a vigorous 'masculine protest', which eventually enabled him to make a heterosexual object choice and to have success in coitus. He now hated his father instead of his mother. The hatred of his father did not spring from the Oedipus complex but was displaced from his mother. There was a trace of Oedipal development and this consisted of his claim that when his mother tried to kill herself by drugs it was he who brought her back to life (a rescue phantasy). Nevertheless, his intense ambivalence towards his mother had to have an outlet. He regretted having saved her because she had had to endure a further terrible year before she died. What there existed of the Oedipus complex lay buried beneath wishes and fears appropriate to the complex of the anal sadism. In this regard it might be said that in his delusion of being a murderer he came as near as he could to playing the part of his father with his mother in intercourse, but the overwhelming power of his passive inclinations immediately rendered him into the mother's role and into the victim of the murderer (the father).

An examination schema

A psychoanalytic examination schema which is both develop-mental and metapsychological in orientation is able to demonstrate the 'organic' continuity which exists between the symptoms of a psychosis and elements of the pre-illness person-ality. It can also point to the childhood mental events which may have contributed to the vulnerability which was latent in that personality.

Metapsychology

The instinctual drives
The psychotic phenomena which spring from disturbances affecting the instinctual drives cannot be easily classified into those which arise from the libido, on the one side, and aggres-sion, on the other. This is because many delusional ideas reveal traces of both libidinal and aggressive drive activity. The expla-nation for this lies in the drive defusion which occurs in the psychoses, exposing an intense ambivalence to love objects.

There are psychotic phenomena which appear to be predo-minantly libidinal in origin, and they must be classified as such. For example, during an acute psychotic attack relating no longer takes place on the basis of object constancy and with instinctual cathexis, which are inhibited in their aims. The libidinal cathexes have developed a primitive quality *pari passu* with the merging of self and object representations. The overwhelming influence of these primitive cathexes is reflected in the omnipotence and the egocentrism which are part of the acute attack whatever the underlying nature of the illness. It is the merging of objects which leads to the fleeting identifications of a 'primary' kind (appersonation) and to externalizations of aspects of the self (transitivistic phenomena, Freeman, 1977).

A further series of phenomena which arise from the instinctual disturbance, and which must be accommodated by the schema, are those which result from the externalization of the primitive libidinal cathexis on to real and phantasy objects. They can assume the role of persecutors, firstly, because they are now omnipotent, and secondly because they have become the repository of unacceptable wishes which have been altered by a drive defusion. A destructiveness is thus imparted to phallic, anal and oral drive derivatives.

It is the libidinal depletion of the self which is instrumental in causing, within the patient, the sense of helplessness, vulnerability and passivity. As Freud (1913) pointed out, this pathological mental condition has as its normal prototype the state of being in love, where the beloved is endowed with the lover's self-love. The beloved may even replace the lover's ego-ideal (Freud, 1921). This comparison between a normal and a pathological mental state is all the more relevant to the present discussion when account is taken of the fact that the persecutor, when he is a known person, turns out to be a former love object.

In the original schema for the psychotic patient (Freeman, 1973b), precedence was given to the way in which the libido is distributed between self and object. However, some sharper distinctions have to be drawn. What is the source of the libido which brings about the hypercathexis of the self? As was shown above, it may come from object representations, but this is not always so, as is illustrated by those cases of mania which follow a depression precipitated by object loss. Here the most likely source of the libido is the 'complex of melancholia' (Freud, 1917) which binds the libido in the identification with the lost object. The schema has to be specific about the changes which affect the quality of the libidinal cathexis. Not only does the libido revert to the primitive narcissistic state but under certain conditions it is 'transformed' into aggression as in the persecutory types of schizophrenia and in paranoiac psychoses.

The problem of schema construction is further complicated by the fact that the merging of self and object, which is at the centre of the libidinal hypercathexis in an acute psychotic attack, does not occur in certain cases, the clinical diagnosis of which can range from paranoid states through narcissistic personality disorders to borderline states or pseudoneurotic schizophrenia. In these cases the outcome of the withdrawal of object libido is a total identification with the object which persists indefinitely, unlike the transient identifications of the acute psychotic attack. The absence of a phase of merging is indicated by the absence of transitivistic phenomena.

Ego and superego
As far as the schema is concerned it has to take account, first, of the phenomena which are the result of a dissolution of the ego and the superego, and, second, of those manifestations of the illness which are the outcome of a reconstruction of these psychical structures. The most common source of material for the section of the schema on reconstruction comes from delusional content. This presents the new pathological object relationships formed on the basis of the self as well as object representations which have taken the place of those which existed prior to the psychosis. Hallucinatory manifestations and disturbances of speech form and content are yet other categories of data resulting from the attempt at reconstruction.

The stability of the reconstructed ego appears to depend on freedom from anxiety (Freeman, 1979). This freedom continues for as long as the defences (reactions, Katan, 1979) which replace repression and reaction formation operate. The defence which inhibits anxiety consists of the withdrawal of cathexis from the object representations belonging to the time of the onset of the psychosis. This decathexis allows denial as well as a kind of repression, the effect of which is to restrict the range of ongoing thoughts and short-term memory.

The reconstruction of the ego which occurs in the persecutory type of schizophrenia leaves the cognitive functions largely unimpaired. The boundaries of the self are largely restored, although not sufficiently so to avoid a confusion of the mental and physical aspects of the self with those of the object (the persecutor). Proof that a reconstruction has taken place is to be found in the identifications which were absent prior to the onset of the psychosis.

The reconstruction has the effect of building into the ego physical and mental characteristics of the former love objects. As a result the patient comes to see himself or herself in a different way. New traits of character appear, including mannerisms belonging to the object. These identifications are to be contrasted with those which occur in the hebephrenic catatonic type of schizophrenia in two important respects. The identifications of the paranoiac group are more stable, and they are resented. There is less stability in the hebephrenic-catatonic type of schizophrenias.

As far as the superego is concerned the effects of dissolution, as in mania, will be recorded under the instinctual and ego sections of the schema. Where there is restoration of the superego, as in the depressed phase of manic depression of the circular type, the self-reproaches are the leading manifestation. It is almost impossible to describe phenomena indicative of a reconstructive trend of the superego in the established case of schizophrenia. The externalization and the fragmentation which took place at the onset of the psychosis appear to maintain themselves throughout the illness, in the form of hallucinations with a critical, supervising or observing content.

Danger situations and conflicts
It is not difficult to identify and then record the danger situations which set in motion the process of symptom formation in psychoses. In some cases the danger consists of sexual wishes from all levels of libidinal development, while in others it is a matter of death wishes which are related to object loss or to a fear of object loss. As ambivalence (Freud, 1911, 1917) and problems of bisexuality stand in the closest relationship to the danger situations and conflicts which occur in psychoses, the schema must allow the portrayal of all the phenomena which are the outcome of the conflict over love and hate and over femininity and masculinity.

Developmental aspects

The developmental section of the schema is concerned with attempting to illustrate the kind of personality in which the psychosis arose, and more importantly with trying to identify the elements which contributed to the formation of this personality. Before undertaking these tasks, however, it is necessary to ascertain whether or not there was progress to heterosexual object choice and to genitality, and if so how far these capacities have been nullified by regression. This is the situation most commonly encountered in depressive and paranoiac psychoses, less often in the schizophrenias where arrests in one or more of the developmental lines (Freud, A., 1965) are the usual state of affairs.

As is well known, a wide range of phenomena presents itself whenever there is any degree of personality dissolution. These phenomena, amongst which may be included the manifestations which spring from the primary process, the free expression of instinctual derivatives, ambivalence and need-satisfying behaviour are common to nearly all psychotic disorders, and therefore must be regarded as non-specific. They certainly throw no light on how or why the patient's personality became vulnerable to a psychosis. Nevertheless they are of great importance because they illustrate how certain instinctual derivatives have had no difficulty in shaking off the transformations which enabled them to play a significant part in the formation of the personality structure. During acute phases of schizophrenic and schizophreniform psychoses, genital exhibitionism and scopophilia find a free expression. This behaviour can be contrasted with the excessive shyness and modesty which characterize the pre-illness personality.

As has been illustrated, the content of psychotic symptoms can be used as material to reconstruct a pre-psychotic phase, and to provide hypotheses about the individual patient's childhood mental development. As in the case presented above, the content of the delusions pointed to a disturbance which had affected the evolution of the sexual instincts. In that case it could be asserted, with some confidence, that a fixation of the libido had taken place during the anal phase, hence the persisting anal erotism.

In other cases the delusional content indicates that the predominant fixation was at the oral phase. Brief reference may be made to the case of a 19-year-old female student who came to believe that a lecturer was in love with her (erotomania). The acute attack occurred some months later, when she was staying with an aunt and uncle for a short holiday. During the first night she had to share a bed with another aunt – a spinster. During the night she had thoughts which preoccupied her a year before, namely, that the world was coming to an end. As the night proceeded she found herself thinking about Adam and Eve – was she Adam or Eve? Was she the snake who had enticed Eve to persuade Adam to eat the forbidden fruit? Next morning she felt frightened. She thought her appearance had changed. She must be Cain reincarnated in herself. She had murdered Abel and eaten him. When she saw her uncle she thought he was Abel, come to life and ready to murder her. This idea was confirmed when he took a knife out from the cupboard. The family were going to kill and eat her. At dinner time she refused to eat because she said eating meat would be equivalent to eating herself. In this case a fixation at the phase of oral sadism made it possible for her wish to possess the penis (masculinity) to find expression in the wish to consume a man and so become a man.

The schema must be so constructed as to include whatever data are available pointing to the disturbances (fixations) affecting the erotogenic zones and the component instincts. It is then important to identify the personality traits which have their basis in an instinct representation which has been subject to transformation. Then to consider how far a fixation has been the determinant of an object choice when it has occurred. Clearly a distinction has to be made between those alterations in instinctual expression which spring from a transformation in the quality of the instinct, as in the case of anal sadism; and those which are the consequence of changes in the aim and object of the instinct representation. A permanent change can result from reversal and projection as well as from reaction formation.

Similarly, the tendency to externalize unwanted wishes, ideas and physical aspects of the self can become the basis of a personality characteristic. None of these changes, including the trend towards the repression of the hostile component of ambivalence, may be entirely successful, so that active residues of the instinct continue to seek an outlet. Only such an explanation provides an understanding of those individuals who hate cruelty yet are irresistibly drawn to read about acts of cruelty. The schema should ideally draw attention to those failures in instinct transformations because they point to a weakness which is finally exposed in the psychotic attack.

Patients whose pre-illness personality is described by Bleuler (Bleuler, M., 1978) as schizoid, are none other than those persons whose instincts have been profoundly altered in the course of their evolution. The developmental approach, embodied in the schema, inevitably raises the question of why these transformations took place. There are individuals who, at an early age, externalize and disown that which has become unacceptable to them. Very young children castigate other infants for 'dirtiness' before coming to acknowledge that they can be equally 'dirty' (Freud, A., 1965). Is this trend to externalize innate? Is it only accentuated in cases where there has been external conflict in childhood? Is it entirely caused by adverse environmental pressures? The schema cannot answer this question, nor is it its task to do so. Its purpose is, firstly, to draw attention to the instinctual transformations which occurred, and, secondly, to identify the possible 'environmental interferences' (Nagera, 1966) which may have played a part in bringing about these changes.

The case of the patient described earlier illustrates how his Oedipal development was interfered with by pregenital influences. His need for revenge, often an element in Oedipal phantasies, was a product of his anal sadism and found its way into a pseudo-Oedipus complex. Under the best circumstances the schema should be able to present an outline of the developmental pathway which the sexual instincts followed in the course of establishing the Oedipus complex, and further to illustrate the faulty turnings which resulted from internal and external obstacles. The symptoms of the acute psychotic attack can again be used to provide material to assist in this reconstruction of the psychical development as it is believed to have occurred in the patient's early childhood.

Even although the predominance of an erotogenic zone or a component instinct, and the reactions to it, interfere with the firm establishment of the phallic phase in the male patient it is not uncommon to encounter phantasies characteristic of the Oedipus complex. Hero and rescue phantasies are quite common in the delusions of schizophrenic patients. The same phantasies appear in women patients, signifying a failure to pass beyond the phallic phase and allow the expression of their femininity. These are the patients who have had an awakening of clitoral excitability during the oral and anal phases of development.

The search for the developmental contributions to psychotic phenomena cannot be confined to childhood alone, and the schema must take this into consideration. Pre- and early adolescence bring to light behaviour, thought and feeling which closely resemble elements of psychotic symptomatology (Freud, A., 1936, 1949, 1958). Affective egocentrism, a need-satisfying attitude to external objects and a blurring of self/object boundaries may be pronounced or barely discernible, depending on the intensity of the adolescent disturbance. Then there is the alternation between a free expression of pregenital wishes, on the one hand, and a vigorous rejection and sometimes harsh renunciation of any kind of bodily pleasure, on the other. This is reminiscent of phases in the course of a schizophrenic illness. Then there is the way in which the adolescent replaces a former affection or regard for his parents by disparagement of them, criticism and even hatred. This is not so unlike the manner in which the schizophrenic patient substitutes hate for love of his parents. All these adolescent manifestations, which are to be understood as the result of the movement to detach libido from the parents, are much intensified in schizophrenic psychoses.

The schema provides the framework for an evaluation of the individual case, but the gathering of the data to build up a profile is a difficult task. It requires a long period of observation by nurses and ancillary workers as well as the psychoanalytically minded psychiatrist. Where a psychotherapeutic treatment can be sustained with the patient, ample opportunities are available to record the data, which will give flesh and blood to the bones of the schema. Otherwise the investigator is confined to what the patient is prepared to say, to his behaviour and to the accounts given of him by relatives, nurses, occupational therapists, social workers and others. The investigator of these cases requires co-operation between all those who have contact with the patient; it cannot be achieved by the psychoanalytic psychiatrist alone.

An outline of a psychoanalytic examination schema

Metapsychological assessment of the psychotic symptomatology

Dynamics: the conflicts discerned in the symptomatology

(i) *The nature of the libidinal component of the conflict:* is the libido pregenital, phallic or genital? Are the libidinal aims active or passive, masculine or feminine? What are the objects of the libido? How far has regression been responsible for the quality of the drive derivatives?

(ii) *The aggressive component of the conflict:* is this reactive to frustration? Is it a consequence of object loss or is it the outcome of a spontaneous 'transformation' of love into hate? What is the object of the aggression?

(iii) *The response to the instinctual derivatives:* is there anxiety and/or guilt? What psychical means are employed to counter the instinctual derivatives? What part, if any, does externalization, displacement, projection, identification (total) and introjection play? What behavioural reactions follow from the instinctual arousal? Is the motor system affected (catalepsy, negativism); are there compulsive manifestations in the spheres of eating, washing, excreting and genital functioning (masturbation, coitus, etc.)?

Economics: alterations in the valuation of the self and others
  (i) Has the libido undergone a radical redistribution between self and objects? Is there a loss of object cathexis (aim-inhibited and instinctual)? Is the libido predominantly concentrated on the self (overvaluation of the self) or is it located in the representations of real or phantasy (delusional) objects (overvaluation of objects)?
 (ii) Has the redistribution of the libido led to a new psychotic (delusional) reality by way of a revival of adolescent and childhood memories and phantasies?

Structural aspects
  (i) *The effect of regression on the ego:* What is the condition of the ego functions – attention, control of motility including sphincter control, speech, thinking, perception, memory? Are they influenced by the primary process? Is the ego differentiated from the object representations and the id (instinctual) derivatives? What is the condition of such ego defences as repression and reaction formation? Is there dissolution of basic personality traits?
 (ii) *The results of reconstruction of the ego:* how have the ego functions been restored? What measures (reactions) are employed against the drive derivative?
(iii) *The effect of regression on the superego:* is it externalized? Has it been fragmented?

Topographic aspects
How far have the conflicts found access to consciousness, and if so in what form?

Developmental aspects

The psychical state obtaining during the pre-psychotic phase
  (i) Are the conflicts of the pre-psychotic phase, arrived at on the basis of reconstruction, the result of regression from a more advanced state of drive and ego functioning?
 (ii) What is the nature of the pre-psychotic conflicts?
(iii) Are there traces of the conflict in the pre-illness personality?

*The effects of fixations and transformations of the sexual instincts
on development*
The questions listed below cannot, in the nature of things, be
given exact, verifiable answers. Some suggestions are possible
using the symptomatology of the psychosis as material for the
reconstruction of the psychical conditions envisaged as occurring
in early childhood.

 (i) Does the symptomatology point to fixations to erotogenic
      zones and to the aims and objects of component instincts?
 (ii) What part was played by environmental events in the
      causation of the fixations and transformations?
(iii) What effect might they have had on drive fusion? Was there
      a continuing infantile ambivalence in the pre-illness person-
      ality?
 (iv) Is there evidence of the instinctual fixations and transfor-
      mations affecting ego and superego development?
  (v) What effect did the fixations have on childhood sexual
      development? Was there a development to the Oedipus
      phase?
 (vi) What consequences did the fixations have on adolescent
      development?

Summary

In this paper a description is given of an examination scheme for
the psychotic patient. The concepts which form the basis of the
scheme enable the psychoanalytic psychiatrist to evaluate the
clinical manifestations in both metapsychological and developmental terms. This becomes increasingly important where the
contact between patient and psychoanalyst develops into a
therapeutic relationship.

References

Abraham, K. (1907a) 'Psychosexual Differences between Hysteria and Dementia Praecox', in *Selected Papers on Psychoanalysis*, London, Hogarth, 1927, pp. 64–79.

—— (1907b) 'On the Significance of Sexual Traumata in Childhood for the Symptomatology of Dementia Praecox', in *Clinical Papers and Essays on Psychoanalysis*, London, Hogarth, pp. 13–20.

—— (1911) 'Notes on the Psychoanalytical Investigation and Treatment of Manic-Depressive Insanity and Allied Conditions', in *Selected Papers on Psychoanalysis*, London, Hogarth, 1927, pp. 137–57.

Allison, R.S. (1962) *The Senile Brain*, London, Edward Arnold.

Annell, A.L. (1971) *Depressive States in Childhood and Adolescence*, New York, Halstead Press.

Anthony, J. and Scott, P. (1966) 'Manic-Depressive Psychosis in Childhood', *J. Child Psychol. Psychiat.* 1: 53–72.

Batchelor, I.R.C. (1964) 'The Diagnosis of Schizophrenia', *Proc. Roy. Soc. Med.* 57: 417–20.

Betlheim, S. and Hartmann, H. (1924) 'Uber Fehlreaktionen bei der Korsakoffschen Psychose', *Arch. für Psychiat.* 72: 275–86.

Bickford, J.A.R. (1955) 'The Forgotten Patient', in the Forgotten Patient Series, *Lancet* ii.

Bleuler, E. (1911) *Dementia Praecox or the Group of Schizophrenias*, New York, International Universities Press, 1955.

—— (1924) *Textbook of Psychiatry*, London, Macmillan.

Bleuler, M. (1978) *The Schizophrenic Disorders*, London, Yale University Press.

Blum, H. (1981) 'Object Inconstancy and Paranoid Conspiracy', *J. Am. Psychoanal. Ass.* 29: 789–814.

Brown, G.W., Monck, E.M., Carstairs, G.M. and Wing, J.K. (1962) 'Influence of Family Life on the Course of Schizophrenic Illnesses',

Br. J. Preventive and Social Med. 16: 55–68.

Brown, G.W. and Wing, J.K. (1974) 'Influence of Family Life on the Course of Schizophrenic Disorders: A Replication', *Br. J. Psychiat.* 121: 241–58.

Burnham, D. (1955) 'Some Problems of Communication with Schizophrenic Patients', *J. Am. Psychoanal. Ass.* 3:67–81.

Bychowski, G. (1952) *Psychotherapy of Psychosis*, New York, Grune & Stratton.

—— (1956) 'Borderline States', *J. Am. Psychoanal. Ass.* 4: 553–4.

Cameron, J.L., Laing, R.D. and McGhie, A. (1955) 'Patient and Nurse', in the Forgotten Patient Series, *Lancet* ii, pp. 27-35.

Chapman, J. and McGhie, A. (1964) 'Echopraxia in Schizophrenia', *Br. J. Psychiat.* 110: 365–80.

Ciompi, L. (1980) 'The Natural History of Schizophrenia in the Long Term', *Br. J. Psychiat.* 136: 413–20.

Critchley, M. (1964) 'Psychiatric Symptoms and Parietal Disease', *Proc. Roy. Soc. Med.* 57: 422–8.

Des Lauriers, A.M. (1959) *The Experience of Reality in Childhood Schizophrenia*, London, Tavistock.

Enoch, M.D. and Trethowen, W.H. (1979) 'De Clerambault's Syndrome', in *Uncommon Psychiatric Syndromes*, Bristol, John Wright.

Ey, H. (1959) 'Unity and Diversity in Schizophrenia', *Am. J. Psychiat.* 115: 706–24.

Federn, P. (1953) *Ego Psychology and the Psychoses*, London, Imago.

Ferenczi, S. (1912) 'On the Part Played by Homosexuality in the Pathogenesis of Paranoia', in *Contributions to Psychoanalysis*, London, Hogarth, pp. 154–84.

Fischer, A.A. (1972) 'Therapeutic Milieu in the Treatment of Schizophrenia: Some Personal and Organizational Conditions Which Determine Success or Failure', in D. Rubinstein and Y.O. Alanen, eds *Psychotherapy of Schizophrenia*, Amsterdam, Excerpta Medica Press, pp. 261–72.

Fleiss, R. (1961) *Ego and Body Ego*, New York, Schulte Publishing Co.

Forrest, A. (1975), 'Paranoid States and Paranoid Psychoses' in A. Forrest and J. Affleck, eds *New Perspectives in Schizophrenia*, Edinburgh, Livingstone, pp. 32–44.

Fraiberg, S. (1952) 'A Critical Neurosis in a $2\frac{1}{2}$-Year-Old Girl', *Psychoanal. Study Child* 7: 173–215.

Freeman, T. (1965) *Studies on Psychosis*, London, Tavistock.

—— (1969) *Psychopathology of the Psychoses*, London, Tavistock.

—— (1973a) 'Some Comparisons between Childhood and Adult Psychosis', in *A Psychoanalytic Study of the Psychoses*, New York, International Universities Press, pp. 297–324.

—— (1973b) 'The Metapsychological Profile Schema', in *A Psychoanalytic Study of the Psychoses*, New York, International Universities Press.

—— (1974) 'Patients with Functional Psychoses: Their Psycho-Social Status after Hospitalization' (unpublished).

—— (1976) *Childhood Psychopathology and Adult Psychoses*, New York, International Universities Press.

—— (1977) 'On Freud's Theory of Schizophrenia', in *Int. J. Psycho-Anal.* 58: 383–8.

—— (1979) 'Clinical and Theoretical Considerations Which Result from Psychotherapeutic Intervention in Schizophrenia', in C. Muller, ed. *Psychotherapy of Schizophrenia*, Amsterdam, Excerpta Medica Press, pp. 19–30.

—— (1981a) 'On the Psychopathology of Persecutory Delusions', *Br. J. Psychiat.* 139: 529–32.

—— (1981b) 'The Psychoanalytic Examination of a Psychotic State', *Int. Rev. Psycho-Anal.* 8: 315–24.

—— (1984a) 'Erotomania and Transference Love', *Analytic Psychopath. and Psychotherapy* 1: 9–20.

—— (1984b) 'A Three-Year Follow-Up of New Patients Referred to a Psychiatric Outpatient Dept and Admitted to Holywell Hospital, Antrim, N. Ireland' (unpublished).

—— (1985a) 'Nosography and Theory of the Schizophrenias', *Int. J. Psycho-Anal.* 66: 237–43.

—— (1985b) 'Psychotherapy and General Psychiatry', *Psychoanal. Psychotherapy*, 1: 19–29.

Freeman, T., Cameron, J.L. and McGhie, A. (1958) *Chronic Schizophrenia*, London, Tavistock.

Freeman, T. and Gathercole, C.E. (1966) 'Perseveration – The Clinical Symptoms in Chronic Schizophrenia and Organic Dementia', *Br. J. Psychiat.* 112: 127–32.

Freeman, T., Kerr, A. and Mannion, P. (1970) 'The Characteristics and Responses to Treatment of Female Patients under 45 Admitted to Hospital on Account of Depressive Symptoms', *Irish Med. J.* 63: 290–2.

Freeman, T., Wiseberg, S. and Yorke, C. (1984) 'Psychoanalytic Psychiatry: Some Past and Present Studies at the Hampstead Clinic', *Bull. Hampstead Cl.* 7: 247–69.

Freud, A. (1936) *The Ego and the Mechanisms of Defence*, London, Hogarth.

—— (1949) 'On Certain Difficulties in the Pre-Adolescent's Relation to his Parents', in *Indications for Child Analysis and Other Papers*, New York, International Universities Press, 1968.

—— (1958) 'Adolescence', *Psychoanal. Study Child* 13: 225–78.

—— (1963) 'The Concept of Developmental Lines', *Psychoanal. Study Child* 18: 24–31.

—— (1965) *Normality and Pathology in Childhood*, London, Hogarth.

—— (1968) Panel Discussion, *Int. J. Psycho-Anal.* 49: 506–7.

—— (1975) Personal Communication.

—— (1979) 'Mental Health and Illness in Terms of Internal Harmony and Disharmony', in *The Writings of Anna Freud*, New York, International Universities Press, vol. 8, pp. 110–18.

—— (1983) 'Problems of Pathogenesis', *Psychoanal. Study Child* 38: 383–8.

Freud, A. and Burlingham, D. (1944) *Infants without Families*, London, Hogarth, 1974.

Freud, A., Nagera, H. and Freud, W.E. (1965) 'Metapsychological Assessment of the Adult Personality: The Adult Profile', *Psychoanal. Study Child* 20: 9–41.

Freud, S. (1888) 'Preface to the Translation of Bernheim's *Suggestion*', in James Strachey, ed. *The Standard Edition of the Complete Psychological Works of Sigmund Freud*, 24 vols. London, Hogarth, 1953–73. vol. 1, pp. 75–87.

—— (1900) *The Interpretation of Dreams, S.E.* 4–5.

—— (1905) 'Fragment of an Analysis of a Case of Hysteria', *S.E.* 7, pp. 3–122.

—— (1908) 'Hysterical Phantasies and their Relation to Bisexuality', *S.E.* 9, pp. 155–66.

—— (1909) 'Family Romances', *S.E.* 9, pp. 235–41.

—— (1911) 'Psychoanalytical Notes on an Autobiographical Account of a Case of Paranoia', *S.E.* 12, pp. 3–82.

—— (1913) *Totem and Taboo, S.E.* 13, pp. ix–161.

—— (1914a) 'Remembering, Repeating and Working Through', *S.E.*

12, pp. 145–56.
—— (1914b) 'On Narcissism: An Introduction', *S.E.* 14, pp. 67–102.
—— (1915a) 'Observations on Transference Love', *S.E.* 12, pp. 157–71.
—— (1915b) 'A Case of Paranoia Running Counter to the Psychoanalytic Theory of the Disease', *S.E.* 14, pp. 261–72.
—— (1915c) 'The Unconscious', *S.E.* 14, pp. 159–215.
—— (1916) 'The Libido Theory and Narcissism', in *Introductory Lectures on Psychoanalysis*, *S.E.* 16, pp. 412–30.
—— (1917) 'Mourning and Melancholia', *S.E.* 14, pp. 237–58.
—— (1918) 'From the History of an Infantile Neurosis', *S.E.* 17, pp. 3–122.
—— (1920) *Beyond the Pleasure Principle*, *S.E.* 18, pp. 3–64.
—— (1921) *Group Psychology and the Analysis of the Ego*, *S.E.* 18, pp. 67–143.
—— (1923) *The Ego and the Id*, *S.E.* 19, pp. 3–66.
—— (1924) 'The Loss of Reality in Neurosis and Psychosis', *S.E.* 19, pp. 183–7.
—— (1940) *An Outline of Psychoanalysis*, *S.E.* 23, 141–207.
Fromm-Reichmann, F. (1939) 'Transference Problems in Schizophrenia', *Psychoanal. Quart.* 8: 143–55.
—— (1947) 'Problems of Therapeutic Management in a Psychoanalytic Hospital', *Psychoanal. Quart.* 16: 325–35.
Frosch, J. (1983) *The Psychotic Process*, New York, International Universities Press.
Glover, E. (1955) *The Technique of Psychoanalysis*, London, Balliere, Tindall Co.
Goldstein, K. (1943) 'Concerning Rigidity, Character and Personality', *Character and Personality* 11: 209–26.
Greenson, R. (1955) 'Borderline States', *J. Am. Psychoanal. Ass.* 3: 543–4.
Henderson, D.K. and Gillespie, R.D. (1969) in I.R.C. Batchelor, ed. *Textbook of Psychiatry*, London, Oxford University Press.
Hill, L.B. (1955) *Psychotherapeutic Intervention in Schizophrenia*, Chicago, University of Chicago Press.
Hoffer, W. (1955) 'Ego Reactions in Cerebral Disease', in *Psychoanalysis: Practical and Research Aspects*, Baltimore, Williams & Wilkins, pp. 55–71.
Hollos, S. and Ferenczi, S. (1925) *Psychoanalysis and the Psychic Disorder of General Paresis*, New York, Nervous and Mental Disease Publishing Co.

Huber, G. (1979) *Schizophrenie*, Springer, Berlin.

Jackson, J. Hughlings (1894) 'The Factors of Insanities', in J. Taylor, ed. *Collected Works of Hughlings Jackson* 2, London, Staples, 1959, pp. 411–14.

Jacobson, E. (1954) 'On Psychotic Identifications', *Int. J. Psycho-Anal.* 35: 102–8.

—— (1967) *Psychotic Conflict and Reality*, London, Hogarth.

Jelliffe, S.E. (1932) *Psychopathology of Forced Movements and the Oculogyric Crises of Lethargic Encephalitis*, New York, Nervous and Mental Disease Publishing Co.

Jones, M.S. (1952) *Social Psychiatry*, London, Tavistock.

Jung, C.G. (1907) 'The Psychology of Dementia Praecox', in H. Read, ed. *Collected Works of C. G. Jung*, vol. 3, London, Routledge & Kegan Paul, 1960.

Kasanin, J.S. (1933) 'The Acute Schizo-Affective Psychoses', *Am. J. Psychiat.* 13: 97–126.

Katan, M. (1950) 'Structural Aspects of a Case of Schizophrenia', *Psychoanal. Study Child* 5: 145–59.

—— (1954) 'The Non-Psychotic Part of the Personality in Schizophrenia', *Int. J. Psycho-Anal.* 35: 119–27.

—— (1959) 'Schreber's Hereafter – Its Building Up and its Downfall', *Psychoanal. Study Child* 14: 314–62.

—— (1960) 'Dream and Psychosis', *Int. J. Psycho-Anal.* 41: 341–51.

—— (1974) 'The Development of the Influencing Apparatus', *Psychoanal. Study Child* 29: 473–510.

—— (1975) 'Childhood Memories as Contents of Schizophrenic Hallucinations and Delusions', *Psychoanal. Study Child* 30: 357–75.

—— (1979) 'Further Explorations of the Schizophrenic Regression to the Undifferentiated State', *Int. J. Psycho-Anal.* 60: 145–76.

Kernberg, O.F. (1967) 'Borderline Personality Organisation', *J. Am. Psychoanal. Ass.* 15: 646–85.

—— (1974) 'Contrasting Viewpoints Regarding the Nature and Psychoanalytic Treatment of Narcissistic Personalities', *J. Am. Psychoanal. Ass.* 22: 255–67.

Kety, S. (1961) 'The Heuristic Aspect of Psychiatry', *Am. J. Psychiat.* 118: 385–94.

Klein, M. (1932) *The Psychoanalysis of Children*, London, Hogarth.

—— (1946) 'Notes on Some Schizoid Mechanisms', *Int. J. Psycho-Anal.* 27: 99–105.

—— (1957) *Envy and Gratitude*, London, Tavistock.

Knight, R.P. (1953a) 'Borderline States', *Bull. Menninger Cl.* 17: 1–12.

—— (1953b) 'Management and Psychotherapy of the Borderline Schizophrenic Patient', *Bull. Menninger Cl.* 17: 139–50.

Kohut, H. (1971) *The Analysis of the Self*, New York, International Universities Press.

Langfeldt, G. (1960) 'Diagnosis and Prognosis of Schizophrenia', *Proc. Roy. Soc. Med.* 53: 1047–55.

Leonhard, K. (1961) 'Cycloid Psychoses – Endogenous Psychoses Which Are Neither Schizophrenic Nor Manic-Depressive', *J. Ment. Sc.* 107: 633–46.

Leyberg, J.T. (1965) 'A Follow-Up Study of Some Schizophrenic Patients', *Br. J. Psychiat.* 111: 617–25.

London, N. (1973) 'An Essay on Psychoanalytic Theory: Two Theories of Schizophrenia', *Int. J. Psycho-Anal.* 54: 169–71, 194.

Lucas, R. (1985) 'On the Contribution of Psychoanalysis to the Management of Psychotic Patients', *Psychoanal. Psychotherapy* 1: 3–17.

Luria, A.R. (1965) 'Two Kinds of Motor Perseverations in Massive Injury of the Frontal Lobes', *Brain* 88: 1–10.

McLeod, K. (1966) Personal Communication.

Main, T.F. (1946) 'The Hospital as a Therapeutic Institution', *Bull. Menninger Cl.* 1: 35–46.

Mandelbrote, B. and Folkard, S. (1961) 'Some Factors Related to Outcome and Social Adjustment in Schizophrenia', *Acta Psychiat. Scand.* 37: 223–30.

Martin, D.V. (1955) 'Institutionalism', in the Forgotten Patient Series, *Lancet* ii, pp. 42–55.

Meissner, W.H. (1978) *The Paranoid Process*, New York, Aronson.

Menniger, K. (1940) 'Psychoanalytic Psychiatry, Theory and Practice', *Bull. Menninger Cl.* 4: 105–21.

Menninger, W.C. (1936) 'Psychoanalytical Principles Applied to the Treatment of Hospitalized Patients', *Am. J. Psychiat.* 93: 347–56.

Nagera, H. (1966) *Early Childhood Disturbances, The Infantile Neurosis and the Adult Disturbances: Problems of a Developmental Psychoanalytic Psychology*, New York, International Universities Press.

Nunberg, H. (1921) 'The Course of the Libidinal Conflict in Schizophrenia', in H. Nunberg, ed. *Practice and Theory of Psychoanalysis*, New York, Mental and Nervous Disease Monographs.

Pao, P.N. (1979) *Schizophrenic Disorders*, New York, International Universities Press.

Piaget, J. (1929) *The Child's Conception of the World*, London, Routledge & Kegan Paul.

Psychotherapy of Schizophrenia (1972) D. Rubinstein and Y. O. Alanen, eds, Amsterdam, Excerpta Medica Press.

Psychotherapy of Schizophrenia (1976) J. Jorstad and E. Ugelstad, eds, Oslo, Universitetsforlaget.

Psychotherapy of Schizophrenia (1979) C. Muller, ed., Amsterdam, Excerpta Medica Press.

Rangell, L. (1956) 'Borderline States', *J. Am. Psychoanal. Ass.* 4: 554–6.

Ratcliffe, R.A.W. (1964) 'The Change in the Character of Admissions in Scottish Mental Hospitals', *Br. J. Psychiat.* 110: 22–7.

Reich, A. (1960) 'Pathologic Forms of Self-Esteem', *Psychoanal. Study Child* 15: 215–32.

Retterstol, N. (1966) *Paranoid and Paranoiac Psychoses*, Springfield, Charles C. Thomas.

Rie, H.E. (1966) 'Depression in Childhood', *J. Amer. Acad. Child Psychiat.* 5: 653–85.

Ritvo, S. and Solnit, A.J. (1960) 'The Relationship of Early Identifications to Superego Structures', *Int. J. Psycho-Anal.* 41: 295–300.

Rochlin, G. (1953) 'Loss and Restitution', *Psychoanal. Study Child* 8: 288–309.

Rosenfeld, H. (1949) 'Remarks on the Relation of Male Homosexuality to Paranoia, Paranoid Anxiety and Narcissism', *Int. J. Psycho-Anal.* 30: 36–47.

—— (1954) 'Considerations regarding the Psychoanalytic Approach to Acute and Chronic Schizophrenia', *Int. J. Psycho-Anal.* 35: 135–40.

Schilder, P. (1924) *Medical Psychology*, New York, International Universities Press.

—— (1939) 'The Psychology of Schizophrenia', in *On Psychoses*, New York, International Universities Press, 1976, pp. 309–29.

—— (1951) 'On Encephalitis', in *Brain and Personality*, New York, International Universities Press, pp. 21–35.

—— (1976a) 'Organic Psychoses', in *On Psychoses*, New York, International Universities Press, pp. 32–6.

—— (1976b) 'Toxic Psychoses', in *On Psychoses*, New York, International Universities Press, pp. 58–63.

Searles, H. (1963) 'Transference Psychosis in the Psychotherapy of

Chronic Schizophrenia', *Int. J. Psycho-Anal.* 35: 135–50.

Sechahaye, M. (1953) *Symbolic Realization*, New York, International Universities Press.

Segal, H. (1951) 'Some Aspects of the Analysis of a Schizophrenic', *Int. J. Psycho-Anal.* 31: 285–97.

—— (1978) *Introduction to the Work of Melanie Klein*, London, Hogarth.

Simmel, E. (1929) 'Psychoanalytic Treatment in a Sanitarium', *Int. J. Psycho-Anal.* 10: 70–82.

Sperling, O. (1944) 'On Appersonation', *Int. J. Psycho-Anal.* 25: 128–31.

Stanton, A.H. and Schwartz, M.S. (1954) *The Mental Hospital*, London, Tavistock.

Stengel, E. (1930) 'Weitere Beiträge zur Kenntniss des postence-phalitischen Blickkrampfes', *Zeitschr. f.d.ges. Neurol. u. Psychiat.* 127: 441–58, quoted by W. Hoffer (1955) *Psychoanalysis, Practical and Research Aspects*, Baltimore, Williams & Wilkins, pp. 56–7.

—— (1935) 'Ueber psychische Zwangsphänomene bei Hirnkranken und ihre Bedeutung für die Lehre von der Zwangsneurose', *Jahrb. f. Psychiat. u. Neurol.* 52: 236–42.

—— (1947) 'A Clinical and Psychological Study of Echo Reaction', *J. Ment. Sc.* 93: 598–612.

—— (1953) 'Introduction to Freud's "Aphasia" (1891)', London, Imago.

Sullivan, H.S. (1932) 'The Modified Psychoanalytic Treatment of Schizophrenia', *Am. J. Psychiat.* 88: 519–29.

Tausk, V. (1919) 'On the Origin of the "Influencing Machine in Schizophrenia"', in R. Fleiss, ed. *The Psychoanalytic Reader*, London, Hogarth, 1950, pp. 31–64.

Thomas, R. (1966) 'Comments on Some Aspects of Self and Object Representations in a Group of Psychotic Children', *Psychoanal. Study Child* 21: 527–80.

Ugelstadt, E. (1975) 'Psychosocial Treatment Alternatives for Long-Stay Schizophrenic Patients', in J. Jorstad and E. Ugelstadt, E., eds. *Schizophrenia 75*, Oslo, Universitetsforlaget, pp. 397–412.

Vaughan, C.E. and Leff, J.I. (1976a) 'The Influence of Family and Social Factors on the Course of Psychiatric Illness', *Br. J. Psychiat.* 129: 125–37.

—— (1976b) 'The Measurement of Expressed Emotion in the Families of Psychiatric Patients', *Br. J. Soc. Clinical Psychol.* 15: 157–65.

Weinstein, E.A. and Kahn, R.L. (1950) 'The Syndrome of Anosognosia', *Arch. Neurol. Psychiat.* 64: 777–86.

Werner, H. (1957) *Comparative Psychology of Mental Development*, New York, International Universities Press.

Wernicke, K. (1906) 'Grundrisse der Psychiatrie', in K. Jaspers (1946) *General Psychopathology*, J. Hoenig and M. W. Hamilton, trans. Manchester, Manchester University Press, 1965.

Whitehorn, J.C. (1952) 'Psychodynamic Approach to the Study of the Psychoses', in F. Alexander and C. Ross, eds. *Dynamic Psychiatry*, Chicago, University of Chicago Press, pp. 255–84.

Wing, J.K. (1985) 'Relapse in Schizophrenia', *Br. Med. J.* 291: 1220.

INDEX

Abraham, K. 3
'acting out in the transference' 99
acute attacks 49, 50, 57, 163, 167, 173
　at onset 16–31
　in schizophrenias terminating in
　　end states 31–4
'adhesiveness of the libido' 104
adjustment reaction 5, 108–9
adolescence 131–3
adualism 9
affects 16, 17, 148–9
aggression 121, 132, 174, 181
agoraphobia 107, 111
alcoholism 4, 5, 88
Allison, R.S. 102
Alzheimer's disease 87, 127
anal erotism 172, 178
anosognosia 102, 103
anxiety 119, 129
anxiety hysteria 3, 49–50, 64, 65, 82,
　172
　neurotic symptoms 107, 114, 115
aphasia 89
appersonation 2, 7–13, 49, 57, 70, 75,
　128
　classification 8–11
　examples 19, 30, 37, 42, 52
asynergia 135
attention 103

Bleuler, M. 14, 15, 59, 62, 64, 149
　classification of appersonation and
　　transitivism 7, 8
borderline state 11, 136–43
brain tumours 4
breast/mother, persecuting 81–3

case material
　borderline state
　　Desmond 136–9

depression
　Arthur 152–5
neurosis
　Doreen 111–13; Muriel
　111; Nora 109–11
persecutory delusions alone
　Ann 33–4, 46; Clare 27–8;
　Don 47; Geraldine 40; Harry
　30; Henry 32; Hilda 32; Joan
　30, 46; Kath 28, 40, 44; Roberta
　46–7; Tom 24, 25, 31–2, 39–40, 76
persecutory delusions preceded by
　erotomania
　Christine 38–9, 43, 55–6, 58,
　60; Emma 23, 38, 50, 52–5,
　58; Eve 43, 59; May 26, 42;
　Nan 23–4, 60; Rachael 27, 67–8
persecutory delusions preceded or
　accompanied by wish (grandiose)
　delusions
　Charles 21–2, 26, 38, 62;
　Deirdre 45–6, 61; Derek
　29–30, 75; Edith 19; Edward
　36–7; Elsie 37–8, 69; Fiona
　41–2, 158; James 18–19, 37, 63;
　Mary 20, 35, 61; Peter 20–1,
　36, 161–2; Robert 29, 31;
　Sheila 22, 38, 84; William 17,
　36, 50–1, 55; Wilson 45, 63
castration anxiety 52, 55, 177, 141, 143
castration complex 113
castration wish 67, 80
catatonia 2, 14, 15
catelepsy 8
cerebral arteriosclerosis 127
cerebral diseases 89, 94, 127
chemotherapy 2, 9, 16, 21, 33
　in treatment of psychoses 145–8,
　150–1, 160, 161, 165
childhood mental life 11, 115–25

child patients 115–25
  comparison with adults 115–21
  overactive 116
chlorpromazine 145, 146
chronicity 38, 145, 151
claustrophobia 107
'complex of melancholia' 152, 156, 174
confabulations 89
conversion hysteria 3, 64, 107, 143

danger situations 176
death wishes 139, 154
decathexis 58, 132, 175
delusional perception 16
delusional phantasies 71, 75, 76
  non-remitting 75, 76
  remitting 75, 76
delusions
  coital 59
  contents 3, 15, 59–64
  homosexuality 63
  murder 61
  pregnancy 59, 60
  rape 59, 60
  saviour 61
dementia
  arteriosclerotic 3, 89, 91, 92, 94
  pre-senile 3, 89, 95, 127
  senile 3, 89, 90, 92, 95, 127
dementia paranoides 14
dementia praecox 14, 15
depression 23, 38
  manic-depressive 151–7
  reactive 4, 5
depressive neurosis 4
developmental achievements
  127–30, 135
developmental theory of psychoses
  126–35
displacement 58, 82, 89, 124, 168
dissolution 49, 54, 132, 162, 164
'double book-keeping' 15, 34
dreams 4, 153–4, 167
  traumatic 98, 100
drug therapy see chemotherapy

echolalia 97
echo phenomena 97, 98, 101, 103
echopraxia 97
echo reactions 100
ego 127–30, 132–3
  boundaries 7
  dissolution 87, 132, 175–6
  perceptive 89, 92
  reconstruction 175–6, 182
  regression 182
egocentrism 70, 89, 108, 173
elation 16
electroshock therapy 153, 155
encephalitis lethargica 87–8
end states 31, 57, 146
envy 50, 62, 63, 148
  in delusional content 16–19, 21,
    27, 31
epilepsy 3, 4
erotomania 2, 20, 36, 60, 80, 178
  and persecutory delusions 23–4,
    26–7, 38–9, 42–4
  'pure' 44
externalization 70, 128
Ey's acute delusional psychosis 16

father 155, 170–2
Ferenczi, S. 3
Freud, A. 5, 12, 126, 134
Freud, S. 5, 77, 86, 126, 149, 174
  concept of repetition compulsion
    104
  on contents of delusions and
    hysterical phantasies 3, 59, 64
  theory of persecutory paranoia 15,
    79, 80
  theory of schizophrenia 14, 57
frustration 73, 108
functional psychoses 4, 5, 93, 126,
  128–9

general paresis 3, 87, 89
group methods 144, 165

hallucinations 8, 55, 92, 127–9, 159,
  160

auditory 16, 129, 167
contents of 15, 88, 129
effect of chemotherapy 145–6, 148
location of 17
hatred 17, 131, 148, 154
hebephrenia 14, 15
Hecker, E. 15
heterosexuality 20, 51, 80
homosexuality 20, 38, 52, 63, 81, 86
female 56–7, 69, 80
male 51, 162
unconscious 86, 130
Huntington's chorea 87, 127
hypercathexis 142, 174–5
hypertension 93
hysterical neuroses 3, 73–4
hysterical personality 65

identification 65, 67, 75, 117, 128, 162
lost object 156, 174
narcissistic 49
pre-psychotic 49–58
primary 9, 10, 13, 132
primitive 11, 49
projective 11
psychotic 49, 57, 58
'impairment of switching' 95, 96, 100, 101
inattention 102, 103
incest 51, 52, 70
phantasies of 60, 68, 74, 160
index of expressed emotion 147
infants 9, 10, 134
instinct distortion 124
instinctual derivatives 177, 181
instinctual drives 173–5
instinctual wishes 129–30, 134
introjection 11
'introjection-projection' mechanisms 7
introversion 66–70, 73, 75, 108–10
ischaemic heart disease 93

Jackson, J. Hughlings 5, 8
jealousy 43, 50, 57, 63, 148

in delusional content 16, 17, 19, 20, 22–4, 27
Jones, M.S. 144
Jung, C.G. 15

Kahlbaum, K. 15
Katan, M. 80, 82, 83, 152
Kernberg, O.F. 142
Klein, M. 10, 11, 81, 82
Korsakov's psychosis 87, 127
Kraepelin, E. 14, 15

Leonhard's anxiety-elation psychosis 16
libidinal cathexis 104, 154, 163, 173, 174
of objects 10–12
libidinal theory 79–81

mania 128
manic attack 7, 10
masturbation 60, 72, 85, 131, 163, 169–70
female 54, 60, 113, 159
male 51–2, 55, 74
revulsion against 94, 124
mental hospitals 149–50
admission wards 4
population 3, 4
readmission 146–7
mentally handicapped 4
merging 9, 10, 12, 13, 175
metapsychological assessment 164, 173–6, 181
misidentifications 90–2, 95, 96
morbid process 92, 94, 120, 135, 148
mother 10, 77, 140–1, 155, 171–2
fear of 85, 138
hatred of 172
identification with 140
merging with 9
mother transference role 82
motility 8, 89, 116, 126

narcissism 67, 71, 132, 134, 142
negativism 8, 31, 43–4, 131, 157

neurotic patient 1–2
neurotic symptoms 107–14
non-psychotic patient 1
nosography 14–15
nurses 145, 149–50, 181

object cathexis 58, 90–1, 143, 156, 162, 182
object choice 67, 73, 75, 134, 177
object constancy 70, 91, 92, 134, 173
obsessional neurosis 107
Oedipal phase 67, 70, 183
Oedipus complex 77, 129, 172, 179–80
organic mental states 87–106, 124, 127, 135

paranoid psychoses 8, 13, 15, 16
  nosographic aspects 14–34
  persecutory delusions in 21–6, 28–31, 37–40, 44–8, 73
paranoid-schizoid position 10–11
paranoid symptom complex 7
parents 131, 133, 137–8
passivity experiences 16, 20, 34, 49, 171
penis envy 67, 80, 85, 86, 113
pentazocine 88
perceptual constancy 91
persecutory delusions 50, 59, 93, 129, 161
  by known member of opposite sex 26–9, 32–3, 41–5, 79–86
  delusions alone 27–9, 44–5
  delusions preceded by erotomania 26–7, 42–4
  delusions preceded or accompanied by wish (grandiose) delusions 41–2
  by known member of same sex 17–26, 31–2, 35–41
  delusions alone 24–6, 39–41
  delusions preceded by erotomania 23–4, 38–9
  delusions preceded or accom-

panied by wish (grandiose) delusions 17–22, 35–8
  by unknown persons or agencies 29–31, 33–4, 45–8
  delusions alone 30–1, 46–8
  delusions preceded or accompanied by wish (grandiose) delusions 29–30, 45–6
persecutory paranoia 15, 79, 81
persecutory symptom complexes 16
perseveration 95, 96, 98, 100–1
personality disorder 5
phallic fixation 140
phantasies 3, 22, 120
  childhood 12
  delusional 71, 75, 76
  erotic 26, 66
  family romance 61, 131, 137
  homosexual 65, 162
  hysterical 3, 64–6
  omnipotent 131
  phallic-Oedipal 71–3
  prostitution 60, 66, 69
  rape 63, 66
phenothiazines 94
Pick's disease 87, 89, 127
post-encephalitic parkinsonism 3
pre-psychotic phase 50, 51, 57, 166–70, 182–3
pre-psychotic personality 12
primary process 58, 82, 127, 134, 177
  in organic mental states 89, 90, 92
profile schemata 164–6
projection 11
projective mechanisms 99
psychoanalysis in treatment of psychoses 5, 144–65
psychoanalytic examination schema 166–83
  developmental aspects 177–81
  metapsychology 173–6
  outline 181–3
psychopathic personality 4
psychoses 2, 5, 7, 8; *see also* paranoid psychoses

descriptive studies 2
developmental psychopathology
130–5
Jacksonian theory of 8
manic-depressive 4
reactive 68
schizophrenic 17–21, 23–6, 29–30,
35–47, 72–3
theory of 11–13
transference 157
treatment 144–65
psychosocial techniques 151
psychotherapy 104, 148, 150, 152,
153
psychotic conflict 129–30
psychotic patient 1–2, 7

rape 63
regression 66–70, 109, 110, 124, 143,
172
effect on ego and superego 182
libidinal 113, 114
psychical 163
Reich, A. 142
relapses 147, 161
remission 2, 145, 165
repetition 105
automatic (involuntary) 4
compulsive 95, 96, 99–101, 104
repetitive phenomena 103
repression 119–20, 154
resistance 1, 64, 119, 152, 158, 163

sadism 85, 170
anal 123, 170, 173, 179
oral 178
sado-masochism 170
Schilder, P. 89–91, 94, 104
schizophrenia 4, 6–9, 14, 15, 31
chronic 8
hebephrenic-catatonic 8, 49–50,
132
negative symptoms 9
non-remitting 157–63
paranoid 8, 13, 73

positive symptoms 9
predisposition 11
pre-psychotic phase 6
remitting 157–63
school phobia 115–16
secondary process 127, 128, 132
self-object discrimination 55, 70, 97
separation fears 122, 123
splitting 14–15
Stengel, E. 88
substitution 82, 83
suicide 41, 45, 141, 153
superego 87, 88, 94, 127–30, 132–3
dissolution 132, 175
reconstruction 176, 182
regression 182
symptom formation 133–4

therapeutic task assessment 163–5
transference 66, 82, 103–5, 138,
149–50, 153
phantasies 117
transference love 2
transitivism 2, 7–13, 49, 57, 70, 73,
120
classification 8–11
examples 18, 20–2, 24, 27, 41, 42,
45, 52, 158
treatment of psychoses 144–65
assessment of therapeutic task
163–5
contribution of psychoanalysis
148–51
manic-depressive depressions
151–7
schizophrenias 157–63

Wernicke, K. 7
wish (grandiose) delusions 2, 16, 17,
20, 25, 50, 61
and persecutory delusions 17–22,
29–30, 35–8, 41–2, 45–6
wish phantasies 64
withdrawal 43–4, 131, 157